101 Learning & Transition Activities

101 Learning & Transition Activities

Bradley Smith and Adam Smith

THOMSON
DELMAR LEARNING™

Australia Canada Mexico Singapore Spain United Kingdom United States

KH

101 Learning and Transition Activities
Bradley Smith and Adam Smith

Vice President, Career Education SBU:
Dawn Gerrain

Director of Editorial:
Sherry Gomoll

Managing Editor:
Robert Serenka

Senior Acquisitions Editor:
Erin O'Connor

Editorial Assistant:
Stephanie Kelly

Director of Production:
Wendy A. Troeger

Production Manager:
J.P. Henkel

Production Editor:
Joy Kocsis

Production Assistant:
Angela Iula

Director of Marketing:
Wendy E. Mapstone

Channel Manager:
Kristin McNary

Marketing Coordinator:
David White

Composition:
Interactive Composition Corporation

Cover Design:
Joseph Villanova

Printed in the United States
1 2 3 4 5 XXX 08 07 06 05

For more information contact Thomson Delmar Learning, Executive Woods, 5 Maxwell Drive, Clifton Park, NY 12065-2919.

Or find us on the World Wide Web at www.thomsonlearning.com, www.delmarlearning.com, or www.earlychilded.delmar.com

Library of Congress Cataloging-in-Publication Data

Smith, Bradley, 1959–
101 learning and transition activities / Bradley Smith and Adam Smith.
p. cm.
ISBN: 1-4180-2070-2
1. Early childhood education—Activity programs.
2. Motor learning. I. Title: One hundred one learning and transition activities. II. Title: One hundred and one learning and transition activities. III. Smith, Adam, 1980– IV. Title.
LB1139.35.A37S65 2006
372.21—dc22

2005026682

NOTICE TO THE READER

Publisher does not warrant or guarantee any of the products described herein or perform any independent analysis in connection with any of the product information contained herein. Publisher does not assume, and expressly disclaims, any obligation to obtain and include information other than that provided to it by the manufacturer.

The reader is expressly warned to consider and adopt all safety precautions that might be indicated by the activities herein and to avoid all potential hazards. By following the instructions contained herein, the reader willingly assumes all risks in connection with such instructions.

The Publisher makes no representation or warranties of any kind, including but not limited to, the warranties of fitness for particular purpose or merchantability, nor are any such representations implied with respect to the material set forth herein, and the publisher takes no responsibility with respect to such material. The publisher shall not be liable for any special, consequential, or exemplary damages resulting, in whole or part, from the readers' use of, or reliance upon, this material.

The author and Thomson Delmar Learning affirm that the Web site URLs referenced herein were accurate at the time of printing. However, due to the fluid nature of the Internet, we cannot guarantee their accuracy for the life of the edition.

8/16/06

From Bradley, to my three children, Adam, Amber, and Aimee: you were my guinea pigs.

From Adam, to all the parents who entrusted me with their children while I was yet a child myself.

Contents

Activity Matrix by Ages and Times

Activity #	Activity Title	Activity Category	Page	Ages	TIMES	
					5–10 min	10+ min
1	Shake It Out, Baby	Large & Small Motor Skills	15	3–7		X
2	Jim's Gym	Large & Small Motor Skills	17	3–7		X
3	Fishin' Hole	Large & Small Motor Skills	19	3–7	X	
4	Make-Over Madness	Large & Small Motor Skills	21	3–7	X	
5	Super Spy Shoe Phone	Large & Small Motor Skills	23	3–6	X	
6	Have a Look at Cookin' with Patsy	Large & Small Motor Skills	25	3–8		X
7	What's All the Racket?	Large & Small Motor Skills	27	3–8		X
8	Put Your Finger on the Wall	Singing—With or Without Actions	31	3–6	X	
9	There Was a Wise Old King	Singing—With or Without Actions	32	3–7	X	
10	The Clean-Up Song	Singing—With or Without Actions	34	3–6	X	
11	The Hokey Pokey	Singing—With or Without Actions	35	3–10	X	
12	The Hand-Washing Song	Singing—With or Without Actions	36	3–6	X	
13	If We All Pick Up Toys	Singing—With or Without Actions	37	3–6	X	
14	There Was a child Who Had a Name	Singing—With or Without Actions	38	3–6	X	
15	Where Is Thumbkin?	Singing—With or Without Actions	39	3–5	X	
16	The Quiet-Time Song	Singing—With or Without Actions	41	3–4	X	
17	Radio Sing-Along	Singing—With or Without Actions	42	3–6	X	
18	The Circle-Time Song	Singing—With or Without Actions	43	3–6	X	
19	Our Class Has Many Children	Singing—With or Without Actions	45	3–6	X	
20	Talking Box	Quiet Down/Crowd Control	49	3–5	X	
21	The Quiet Game	Quiet Down/Crowd Control	51	3–4	X	
22	I'm Looking for a Volunteer Who . . .	Quiet Down/Crowd Control	52	3–6	X	
23	I Spy with My Little Eye	Quiet Down/Crowd Control	53	3–7	X	
24	Let's Sneak Up on the Other Class	Quiet Down/Crowd Control	54	3–6	X	
25	Who's in the Closet?	Quiet Down/Crowd Control	55	3–6	X	
26	Questions About a Missing Person	Quiet Down/Crowd Control	57	3–8	X	
27	Everybody Point!	Quiet Down/Crowd Control	59	3–8	X	
28	Make-Believe Story Land	Quiet Down/Crowd Control	61	3–10		X
29	Let's Write (or Tell) a Story	Quiet Down/Crowd Control	63	3–12	X	
30	Mouth Full of Bubbles	Quiet Down/Crowd Control	65	3–6	X	

Activity #	Activity Title	Activity Category	Page	Ages	TIMES 5–10 min	10+ min
31	Soldiers on Parade	Quiet Down/Crowd Control	67	3–8	X	
32	Make-Believe Chewing Gum	Quiet Down/Crowd Control	69	3–8	X	
33	What Sound Does the Wind Make?	Quiet Down/Crowd Control	71	3–6	X	
34	Quiet or Loud	Recognition/Memory	75	3–10	X	
35	Up or Down	Recognition/Memory	77	3–8	X	
36	In or Out	Recognition/Memory	78	3–5	X	
37	Ring Around the Rosie	Recognition/Memory	80	3–6		X
38	What Did You Do This Past Weekend?	Recognition/Memory	82	3–12		X
39	What Do You Want for Christmas? (or your Next Birthday)	Recognition/Memory	84	3–12		X
40	Where Do You Want To Go on Vacation?	Recognition/Memory	86	3–12		X
41	Line Up by Color	Recognition/Memory	88	3–10		X
42	Line Up by Clothing	Recognition/Memory	89	3–10		X
43	Line Up if You Can Tell Me Something	Recognition/Memory	90	3–10		X
44	Animal High-Dive Competition	Recognition/Memory	92	3–5		X
45	Miniature Car Wash Rampage	Recognition/Memory	94	3–4		X
46	Body Drawing	Recognition/Memory	96	3–4	X	
47	Drawing Things	Recognition/Memory	98	3–6		X
48	Random Office Supply Highlight	Recognition/Memory	100	3–5	X	
49	A Visit from Our Friendly Pet . . . Whatever	Recognition/Memory	101	3–6		X
50	Cheer for the Monkey	Recognition/Memory	103	3–5	X	
51	Winter or Summer?	Recognition/Memory	105	3–5	X	
52	Name That Thing	Recognition/Memory	107	3–6	X	
53	Name That Shape	Recognition/Memory	109	3–6	X	
54	Missing Person	Recognition/Memory	111	3–6	X	
55	Just What Do You Think You're Wearing, Young Lady?!	Recognition/Memory	113	3–6		X
56	Scrub-a-Dub Time	Recognition/Memory	115	3–6	X	
57	Elvis and the Animals	Repetition	119	3–8	X	
58	Name That Class	Repetition	122	3–8	X	
59	Last Night for Dinner, I Had . . .	Repetition	123	3–10	X	
60	Today When I Woke Up, I . . .	Repetition	124	3–10	X	
61	Doctor Dentist	Character Sketch/Role-Play	127	3–6		X
62	Doctor Doctor, Give Me the News	Character Sketch/Role-Play	129	3–6		X
63	Mr. X-ray Picture Guy	Character Sketch/Role-Play	131	3–8		X
64	Is My Medicine Ready Yet?	Character Sketch/Role-Play	133	3–6		X
65	I Think There's Something Wrong with My Car	Character Sketch/Role-Play	136	3–6		X
66	My Toilet Won't Flush	Character Sketch/Role-Play	138	3–6		X
67	My House Needs To Be Fixed	Character Sketch/Role-Play	140	3–6		X
68	Could You Use a Loan?	Character Sketch/Role-Play	142	3–6		X
69	Are You Going To Eat Those Fries?	Character Sketch/Role-Play	144	3–6		X
70	Why Don't You Try a Size 72?	Character Sketch/Role-Play	146	3–6		X
71	Thanks for Calling Smith, Smith, Johnston and Smith	Character Sketch/Role-Play	148	3–8		X
72	Hey, Your Yard is on Fire!	Character Sketch/Role-Play	150	3–8		X
73	How Fast Were You Going?	Character Sketch/Role-Play	152	3–8		X

Activity #	Activity Title	Activity Category	Page	Ages	TIMES 5–10 min	10+ min
74	Atten-HUT!	Character Sketch/Role-Play	154	3–8		X
75	Could I Get You a Pillow or Some Peanuts?	Character Sketch/Role-Play	156	3–8		X
76	Off We Go Into the Wild Blue	Character Sketch/Role-Play	159	3–8		X
77	May I Give You a Lift?	Character Sketch/Role-Play	161	3–8		X
78	The Wheels on the Bus . . . Are My Job	Character Sketch/Role-Play	163	3–8		X
79	Come on Back . . . Okay . . . a Little More	Character Sketch/Role-Play	166	3–8		X
80	Big Wheels a 'Rollin'—No, I mean BIG WHEELS	Character Sketch/Role-Play	169	3–8		X
81	Fresh Bread	Character Sketch/Role-Play	171	3–6		X
82	How Do You Like Your Steak?	Character Sketch/Role-Play	173	3–8		X
83	Coffee, Tea, or Milk?	Character Sketch/Role-Play	175	3–8		X
84	How Fast Can You Type?	Character Sketch/Role-Play	178	3–8	X	
85	Vote for Me—I'm a Nice Guy	Character Sketch/Role-Play	180	4–10	X	
86	Your Honor, My Client is Innocent!	Character Sketch/Role-Play	182	4–10		X
87	This Was a Good Person	Character Sketch/Role-Play	184	6–10	X	
88	Where Do You Want Those Trees?	Character Sketch/Role-Play	186	3–8	X	
89	Red Curtains Will Look Just Right	Character Sketch/Role-Play	188	3–8	X	
90	How Many Hats Does a Farmer Wear?	Character Sketch/Role-Play	190	3–6	X	
91	I Wouldn't Put a Wall There	Character Sketch/Role-Play	193	3–6		X
92	Pal, Don't Drink the Poison!	Character Sketch/Role-Play	195	3–8		X
93	We're Going to the Store	Imagination	199	3–6		X
94	If You Were an Animal, What Would You Be?	Imagination	201	3–6	X	
95	We're Going to Work	Imagination	202	3–7		X
96	Let's Ride the Subway	Imagination	204	3–10	X	
97	Let's Take a Taxi to the Airport	Imagination	206	3–8	X	
98	Tell Me How To Get to Grandma's House	Imagination	208	3–7		X
99	Where's My Chicken?	Imagination	210	3–7		X
100	Just a Minute . . . I'm in the Shower	Imagination	212	3–7	X	

Preface

For most of my life, I have been an observer of children, parents, and teachers. A few years ago I began noticing some similarities in the people I was observing—specifically in adults' expectations toward children. Adults almost always expected children to be able to make transitions easily from one activity, or from one place, to another. (I'm over 40 and have difficulty doing that myself!) Sometimes this simply reflects adults' laziness or hurry. More often, though, it reflects adults' not understanding children's needs and motivations, an outgrowth of their not being trained or equipped to provide for these needs.

By the time we are adults, we usually have developed a clear understanding of what we are doing and why—but children have not. Even though children do not share our wealth of knowledge and experience, we unthinkingly expect them to make transitions with little or no explanation or preparation for the changes in their lives. We don't realize the effects that even minor change can have on children, especially very young children. What to us may be a simple matter of moving from point A to point B may be a major transition for a child.

When my son Adam—now my adult co-author—was a child, I watched, curious, as he learned early to occupy himself. What a vivid imagination! As a parent, I could have—and maybe should have—helped him more by introducing transition activities, but Adam had an uncommon ability to come up with transition activities on his own. Some children do this instinctively, and other children do not. Over the years, I have watched Adam as he was working with children. His uncanny ability, as a teacher, to create something out of nothing has entertained hundreds of children while they were transitioning.

As a result, I sensed a need for training and equipping parents and caregivers to help children with transitions. In this handbook, Adam and I have combined our talents, abilities, and energies to create transition and learning activities for children. We hope that you will enjoy and benefit from our offering—to the ultimate benefit of children. As you put the principles of this book into action, we are confident that your frustration level as a parent or teacher will dissipate.

The activities in this book are geared to children ages three–ten years. The activities suggest the most appropriate ages, which may vary depending on the children's innate ability and the teacher's or parent's ability to adapt the activities to a specific age group. Some activities might be over a three-year-old's head, and others too immature for a ten-year-old. We have "field-tested" most of these activities successfully for the suggested ages. Age-appropriateness and the nature of each activity should remain at the discretion and direction of the adult who is leading the activity. Happy transitioning!

Bradley Smith

The editors at Thomson Delmar Learning thank the following reviewers for their time, effort, and thoughtful contributions, which helped to shape the final text:

Julie Bakerlis, MS
Quinsigamond Community College
Worcester, MA

Heather Fay
Early Childhood Education Consultant
Akron, OH

Mary Hornbeck
Special Beginnings Early Learning Center
Lenexa, KS

Dawn Hove, M.P.A.
University of Nebraska-Omaha Child Care Center
Omaha, NE

Jody Martin
Crème de la Crème
Greenwood City, CO

Brenda Schin
Private Child Care Provider and Consultant
Ballston Spa, NY

About the Authors

Bradley Smith has been an adult educator and motivational speaker for more than 20 years. In 1998 he founded HandPrint Productions, a training and consulting firm specializing in small business issues, human resource strategies, leadership, child care center management, and classroom procedures. Bradley has authored a series of 22 video training kits, a six-book policies-and-procedures system for child care centers and, now, the book *101 Transition and Learning Activities.*

Adam Smith has been a creative force in youth and children's educational arenas for more than a decade. In 2002 he founded Headscratch Films and Design, a small production company known for modern print design, independent filmmaking, innovative marketing, and creative teaching solutions. Adam's imaginative perspective, innovative spirit, and humorous storytelling approach enable him to transform even the most mundane teaching into an exciting interactive experience. Adam has written several screenplays and short stories, in addition to co-authoring this book, *101 Learning and Transition Activities.*

Introduction: What Is a Transition Activity?

By this point, you probably are asking yourself, "Just what *is* a transition activity?" Simply put, a transition activity is what takes place between two activities. Sometimes this is merely dead space—or at least we think it's dead space. When working with children, though, dead space usually doesn't stay dead!

A transition activity can be what we do while we are walking down the hall from one room to another. It can be what parents do to entertain children while they are in the car. It can be what takes place between clean-up and circle time. In short, a transition activity is any activity that takes place between two activities.

Some of you are surely thinking: Why can't children sit and wait patiently while mom drives the car across town . . . while the teacher walks them down the hall . . . while Ms. Johnson puts away the centers and readies the art activity? The answer is obvious: Children have a short attention span. Transition activities are needed to provide learning and positive interactions while children are moving from one activity to another.

The younger the children, the more they need transitions. The attention span of children is approximately a minute for each year of their life. Thus, a three-year-old will have about a three-minute attention span and a five-year-old will have about a five-minute attention span. But the attention span is applicable only if the children have something on which to fix their attention. Fifteen-year-olds are able to sit and twiddle their thumbs for five or 10 minutes, but we cannot expect two- or three-year-olds to keep their attention on nothing for any length of time. Children need transition activities on which to focus and to keep them from finding their own unproductive or even potentially dangerous ways to avoid boredom.

Moving from activity one to activity two, or from point A to point B, is unsettling to some children more than others These children act almost as if their world is coming to an end when one activity ends and another one is about to begin. As adults, we have a responsibility to provide them with the transitions they need so they can feel secure during these times of change.

Finally, transition activities can be positive experiences for the adults as well. I say, "If you don't put on a program for the children, they will put one on for you—and the program they put on won't be fun!" Children and adults alike experience the effects when transition activities are lacking. The children are bored or anxious because they are waiting with nothing to do, and the adults are frustrated because the children certainly aren't sitting still and more likely are engaging in rough-and-tumble roughhousing or running around the room throwing things. A word to the wise teacher and parent: Plan for transition times so you and the children can both benefit from them.

Seven Elements of Good Transition Activities

1 Preparation

Parents and childhood educators often are unaware of the need to plan for children's transitional moments throughout the day. Beyond that, the difference between a chaotic transition and a successful transition is how well you anticipate and prepare for the transition. It has been said that "failing to plan is planning to fail." Transitional times go as smoothly as you have planned for them.

Children are not little adults—so you shouldn't expect them to act like adults. Overactive three-year-olds probably won't do well if they are expected to sit still for a long time or to be quiet standing in a single-file row for 10 to 15 minutes while awaiting the next activity. Chances are that a child will get restless, and before you know it, the whole group will follow. Thorough preparation is a good step in warding off the chaos, disorganization, and discipline problems during transitional times.

Practical Tips

- *Maintain a file folder or a card file of transitional activities.*
- *Prepare transitional activities in advance as anticipated for specific daily transitions.*
- *Have one to three extra transitional activities prepared and ready to go at all times—just in case.*

2 Variety

The temptation is to find one or two activities that work and to repeat them again and again. Overdoing any activity, regardless of its worth or effectiveness, will result in the children's becoming restless and uninterested. When children get restless, they start picking on each other and wrestling around, and someone may get hurt. It is important to rotate a variety of creative activities that will maintain the students' interest and attention, keeping them focused on attentively learning.

Practical Tips

- *Constantly keep your eye out for new transitional activities.*
- *Remain open-minded to new ideas and innovations. Don't hesitate to change your transitional activities from week to week or even from day to day.*
- *Set up a rotation schedule for your transitional activities, repeating the activities that the children most enjoy.*
- *Throw out the activities that don't engage the children's interest—but don't throw them too far. They might work with another group or at another time.*

3 Repetition

Repetition, in this context, is not the opposite of "variety," and it does have its own place. You will need transition activities at differing times, and often a time like this will come when you least expect it. It is one of those times when something didn't go exactly as planned or a previous activity didn't take the full amount of time you had planned. In these instances, variety is a premium.

Balancing these are the transition times that are planned into your regular schedule—the times by which you could almost set your clock. You know they are coming, and you know exactly when that will be: pre-nap time, toy pick-up time, getting ready for lunch time, and so on. There can be great wisdom in consistently using the same activity to signal this transition, such as "The Clean-Up Song" or a finger play of some kind. Repetition in transition can give children a sense of security because it reminds them that although change is coming, they know what to expect.

Practical Tips

- *Even as you build these activities into your schedule and repeat them, keep your eyes open for new activities. You might come up with something even better!*
- *Stay alert to the children's reactions. When they show signs that an activity is no longer effective, it is a signal to find something new.*

Enthusiasm

If you are uninterested in an activity, you will convey this attitude to the children. Their enthusiasm for an activity is a reflection of yours. If an activity isn't interesting enough for them, they will find ways to entertain themselves—getting up and running around the room, or worse! If you are enthused and appear visually and verbally excited, the children's attention will much more likely remain on you and the activity itself won't function as a mere time-filler. It will become a fun and energetic learning experience to which the children will willingly devote their time and attention.

Practical Tips

- *Be positive.*
- *Smile.*
- *Use voice inflections, big hand gestures, and exaggerated facial expressions. Overact and be bigger than life itself.*
- *Emotionally buy into what you are doing.*
- *Be willing to be silly.*

Interaction

As adults, we can recall having a hard time paying attention to a person lecturing in a monotone in front of us or rambling on about something. Children should be expected to be even less attentive. If you don't give them an opportunity to interact, they will create opportunities to do some interacting of their own. When adults get bored, we might sit quietly and daydream, or maybe drift into a little cat nap. Children will let you know they are bored by finding an activity that doesn't bore them—which may not be in anyone's best interest.

What if adults were to exhibit child-like expressions of boredom? Try screaming, "I want to play outside!" as loud as you can during your boss' lecture at your next staff meeting, and watch the reaction . . . or maybe not. The lesson to take from this scenario is that interaction helps to maintain a child's attention and also is a proven way of magnifying a child's ability to learn and maintain information. Studies show that most children learn new information best through interactive, hands-on means.

Practical Tips

- *Ask questions.*
- *Use children as volunteers.*
- *Have the children mirror your actions or repeat things you say.*
- *Use interactive props and act out things together.*
- *Reinforce the children for their creativity or how successfully they have completed the activity.*

6 Timing

Timing is everything. Decisions on when to do an activity and how long to carry it out are nearly as important as what activity to do and how to do it. Children have a short attention span, and the younger the child, the shorter the attention span. For that matter, any good activity with any age group, if stretched beyond its time, will become boring and less than entertaining to the participants.

Even an excellent activity will fail if it is done at the wrong time. If students have been sitting inside a stuffy classroom for six hours, having just partaken of a triple chocolate birthday cake and a sugar-loaded drink, the "Quiet Game" is not the recommended transitional activity for that time. To be most effective, the appropriate activity must be placed in a time slot in which it will capture the attention of its participants.

Practical Tips

- *In general, follow the suggested amount of time allotted to each activity.*
- *Be aware of the overall mood and tone of your class at all times. If an activity is going extremely well, extend it a bit—but don't overdo it. If an activity isn't going well at all, cut it short and move on.*
- *Plan activities that relate to other learning objectives or activities to support and enhance the experiential learning.*

7 Age-Appropriateness

Children's ability to mentally comprehend an activity often determines how much attention they give it. Different age groups comprehend on different levels and enjoy different activities. You can assume that sixth-grade students won't enjoy a video of a big purple dinosaur hopping and dancing around in circles singing about the colors on its bright big bouncy beach ball. Or that a complicated lecture on mathematical equations will not be understood and appreciated by a group of two-year-olds (or sixth-graders, for that matter).

Whatever the creativity and validity of an activity, it will not be effective with an inappropriate age group. To achieve the best results, we must cater to the students' level of understanding and areas of interest without compromising essential learning objectives.

Practical Tips

- *In choosing specific activities, follow the age recommendations suggested here.*
- *Familiarize yourself with the average learning and comprehension skill, conception level, and recreational interests of the age group with which you are working.*
- *Read up on age-appropriate activities, and use what you learn to observe your students.*

Seven Types of Transition Activities

Large Motor and Small Motor Skills

Emphasizing large and small motor skills through active transition activities has a threefold purpose:

1. Active transition activities enhance hand/eye coordination and dexterity.
2. They act—as all transition activities do—as a filler to keep the children occupied between other activities or while the children are transitioning between areas or geographical places.
3. They give the children an opportunity to be active and burn off excess energy. Children, by nature, can't sit still all the time. We would be worried if they did.

Parents and teachers recognize that there are times when a child needs more movement or activity. Sometimes a teacher realizes this in the middle of a lesson. At that moment, there are three choices: Scrap the whole thing and go on to something different; go ahead with the activity but without the attention of the whole group; or take a short break and promote some motor activity.

Think for a moment. Even when you, as an adult, go to a seminar, church, or most other groups, you have opportunities every 15–45 minutes to at least stand up, and often to move around. Why is this so? An old speaker's motto advises that "the mind can grasp only what the seat can endure." Translated, this means that people will mentally check out if you make them sit still too long.

If this is true for adults, how much more it is true for children! Remember the attention span formula: 1 minute of attention span for every year of the child's age. Therefore, if you have a group of two-year-olds, you need to change the pace in some way every 2 minutes.

This book includes seven activities involving large motor and small motor skills. Two of these are "Shake It Out, Baby," in which the children, beginning at the head and ending at the toes, shake out all those fidgets; and "What's All the Racket?" in which the children devise their own rhythm band. As with most of the activities in this book, props aren't necessary. In some cases they can be introduced to enhance the activity but are not required to complete it.

You can pull these activities out of your bag of tricks any place at any time you sense that the children are getting restless. Maybe you will want to join in. Adults shouldn't always sit still either!

Singing—With or Without Actions

Even though research has shown conclusively that children benefit from being exposed to music, parents and teachers in my observation are faced with "feast or famine" in this regard. If you, as a parent or a teacher, aren't exposing your children to music, you're doing them a disservice.

Music is an easy, go-anywhere activity. You can expose children to music by playing it in the background while they are engaged in other activities. I have observed adults' having the television on to provide background sound, but music is a better "filler" and isn't distracting because it doesn't require visual or other sensory input. Also, music can be used to enhance children's imagination. Prior to the advent of television and other electronic formats, children listened to radio programs—popular music, children's programming, drama with a music background—which required them to use their imagination (just as reading does). Music encourages imagination.

When exposing children to music, don't get stuck on only one type of music. Don't play only "children's music" or set a radio to a Top 40 rock station. Expose children to a wide range of classical music, classic rock, big band, jazz, blues.

When you add actions, the music also can be considered as a large and small motor transition activity. When developing actions to accompany the music, don't feel compelled to come up with "cutesy" hand, arm, and leg motions that try to draw a picture of the song. Although there's nothing wrong in doing this, take it to the next level by having the children move and dance to the music. Music and dance allow the children to express emotions beyond the basic motor activity.

Examples can be as simple as singing along with a tune on the radio, as in the "Radio Sing-Along" activity, or as complex as doing "The Hokey Pokey." We have provided 12 suggestions, but you are only as limited as your knowledge of music. And if your knowledge is limited, this category offers a great opportunity to learn together.

Quiet Down/Crowd Control

Quiet-down activities are intended to do just that— to help the children settle down. Not all transition activities are quiet-down activities, but there's a time when the children need to be quiet, and for these times you should be able to call upon a gaggle of good quiet-down activities.

At other times, children need a structured opportunity to be loud and "blow-off steam" for a few minutes. Actually, these activities increase the effectiveness of the quiet-down activities because the children will have had an opportunity to burn off that extra energy.

Sometimes quiet-down activities are needed as a follow-up to other types of transition activities. Or you may want to introduce an activity to return to your original or next activity. Because you are changing gears every 2 to 5 minutes, you won't mind in the least doing a transition activity followed by another transition activity.

Quiet-down activities are intended first to get the children's attention, and then to calm down, slow down, and quiet down. The activity can be something as simple as a series of hand claps for which children are taught to listen. Whenever they hear this type of hand clap, they know they are to respond by joining in the clap and then pay attention to the teacher or adult in charge.

The 14 quiet-down activities in this book range from "I'm Looking for a Volunteer Who . . . ," which is brief and asks the children specifically to be quiet; to "Everybody Point!" in which you ask the children to point to items you mention, instead of talking; to "Let's All Write (or Tell) a Story," which is intended for older children who can write. From this starting point, you no doubt will invent many other quiet-down activities.

Recognition/Memory

Recognition activities are intended to expand children's knowledge, enhance their memory, and help them recognize concepts or objects around them. The suggested age range for the activities in this book is three to ten years. The recognition/memory activities are especially good for young children between ages two and five years, but you could adapt this type of activity for students in middle school, too, using more complicated concepts.

Some variations for older children might be to find geometric shapes in signs, symbols, or buildings when on a fieldtrip. The older the children, the more complex the objects they would be required to find, such as a triangle or an equilateral triangle, or a square versus a dodecahedron.

Examples of the 23 activities in this category are: "In or Out," which deals with the concept of opposites; "Body Drawing," in which the children are to recognize parts of the human body; or "Missing Person," in which they try to identify who is missing from their group.

Repetition

In the Repetition category, the children repeat and add to specific information as a memory-enhancing activity that will help them concentrate and engage the memory center of the brain. There are four activities, and it's an easy category for you to expand upon. "Elvis and the Animals" consists of a story the teacher or parent tells that asks children to repeat names of the series of animals; and "Today When I Woke Up, I . . . ," in which the children each offer their contribution and the group must try to remember all of the responses as they go along.

This category of activity is good for younger children, and it can be adapted for older children as well. Use your creative mind to think of additional repetitive activities that will interest the children while being mind-expanding. And who knows? Maybe the repetitive transition activities will improve your memory as well!

6 Character Sketch/Role-Play

In character sketch and role-play activities, the children are encouraged to watch or be involved in a role-play type of interaction. This might include a teacher (or a visitor for that matter) dressing up as a character and acting out a role. A child or a group of children might be asked to role-play their understanding of a specific scenario, which can be highly educational in nature—or simply something that is silly or fun.

This type of transition activity involves a lot of pretending. Most of the activities in this category also are qualified to be in the Imagination category, described next. What makes these activities unique is that the imagination stems from a character sketch or a specific role-play. As examples, "Doctor Doctor, Give Me the News" is a role-play of a visit to the doctor; "Are You Going To Eat Those Fries?" gives children an opportunity to run their own imaginary fast food restaurant; and "May I Get You a Pillow or Some Peanuts?" takes the children on an imaginary airplane ride.

This category has more activities than any other category in this book—32 to be exact. Although most of these activities do suggest possible props, you could do them anywhere with no props at all. The description and detail for each of these activities will be determined by the age group. For younger groups, description should be less, replaced by more interaction and role-play.

Imagination

Transition activities require the most creativity on the part of the teacher or parent, as well as the children. In these activities you will lead the children into an imaginary world where anything is possible. Your only limitation will be your ability to get "out of the box" and imagine, pretend, and just be crazy. We offer eight of these activities, two of which are, "We're Going to the Store," in which the children pretend to go to the grocery store, complete with the drive and the walk to and from the car; and "Just a Minute . . . I'm in the Shower," in which the children take an imaginary shower (with their clothes on, of course).

These types of activities rarely call for any props and could be done anywhere at any time. They are well-suited to riding in the car because most can be done even while strapped into a seatbelt.

Large and Small Motor Skills

The activities in this category are intended to:

- Enhance hand/eye coordination and dexterity.
- Act as a "filler" to keep children occupied between other activities or while they are transitioning between places or locations.
- Provide an opportunity for the children to be active and burn off excess energy.
- Be done without props, although they can provide enhancement in some cases.

Shake It Out, Baby

Objective
To use large and small motor skills while learning the body parts

Approximate Time
5–15 minutes

Ages
3–7

Required Materials
NONE

- Have the children stand up in a straight line and "freeze."
- Tell them you were outside in the rain, tripped and fell into a puddle, and got soaking wet.
- Say that you have to dry off but you don't have a towel, so you have to shake yourself like a dog. Ask the children if they have ever seen a dog shake off water.
- Have all the children join you as you demonstrate how to shake off the water.
- Now tell the children, "We have to get the water off our hands. Shake them really fast and jittery!"
- Repeat for the feet, hair, and other body parts (even tongues, ears, tummies, etc.)—including two or more body parts at the same time.
- As the activity nears an end, have the children go through the body parts really fast, not giving them much time to do each part.

(continues)

Shake It Out, Baby *(continued)*

Practical Tips

- *Make sure that the children have enough room to shake and move in their own individual spot. Use the whole room for this transition.*
- *As an enhancement, play a recording of that old song "Twist and Shout" while you all shake, shake, shake!*

Jim's Gym

Objective
To exercise and promote large and small motor skills

Approximate Time
5–15 minutes

Ages
3–7

Required Materials
A whistle
A stereo with upbeat music

- Use this activity on rainy days to give children a chance to release some energy.
- Have the stereo off to the side ready to go.
- Place the whistle around your neck and dress up (or have someone else dress up) as an exercise trainer (sweatshirt and sweatpants; maybe stuff some toilet paper in your sleeves to make it look as if you have bulging muscles).
- Have the children stand up along a taped line on the floor.
- Introduce stretching exercises: arms up to the ceiling, out to the sides, and down to touch the toes; fingers up and down, all five fingers at once, and one at a time.
- Have the children roll their neck back and forth and side to side as you demonstrate.
- Have them stretch their mouth wide open and closed, then their eyebrows up and down.
- Ask the children to wiggle their ears, clench their teeth, stretch their tongue, and practice fake "gargling."
- Take them through each stretch again, one by one, step by step.

(continues)

Jim's Gym *(continued)*

- Now turn on the music and lead them in basic aerobic exercises such as jogging in place.
- Have the children run as fast as they can, then slow, then fast again, and so on.
- Vary the routine when you repeat the activity later by doing jumping jacks, windmills, hopping in place, clapping fast and slow, moving the arms up and down at different speeds, or any other aerobic variation you think the children would enjoy.

Practical Tips

- *Use this activity to alleviate some of the closed-in, antsy atmosphere of an "indoor day."*
- *Use the whistle to bring the children back to attention if they get too loud or out-of-control.*
- *Try this transition when children need to burn off excess energy and are all wound up before a nap. Keep it up until you wear them out. Then do a calm-down activity to quiet them before naptime.*

3

Fishin' Hole

Objective
To develop large and small motor skills

Approximate Time
5–10 minutes

Ages
3–7

Required Materials
Your imagination!

- Tell the children you're all going on a fishing trip, and ask them what things they need to bring along.
- Help them make a list: fishing pole, worms, hooks, fishing boat, hip boots, fishing hat, cooler full of drinks and sandwiches, and other fishy stuff.

- Have the children act as if they're getting dressed for their special fishing outing. Go through the actions of putting on a fishing hat and pulling on hip boots and their favorite fishing vest with all the hooks on it, and so on.
- Help them pretend to gather up all the items you have on your list. You might have different children be responsible for different items (or pretend to be trying to carry too many items and continually dropping them).
- Have the children act as if they are climbing into the fishing boat and starting the engine, including the sound of the engine starting.
- Drive the boat out into the best fishing spot (you'll find it by using your "Official Imaginary Genuine Imitation Fish Finder Thingy 2002"

(continues)

Fishin' Hole *(continued)*

because it's the best imaginary fish-finder on the market).

- Have the children get out their fishing pole, put the squirmy worm on the hook, and cast the line out into the lake.
- Wait until they've snagged something, then have them reel in the line.
- Repeat the cast–reel action until finally, on the last cast, you act as if you get a bite (you might even lose your worm a few times and have to re-string one).
- Have all the children reel in their enormous 3-ounce bass as fast as they can.
- When all the fish have been reeled in, have the children hold their catch as high as they can so you can take their picture.
- Go to each child and take a quick "snapshot."
- If you know anyone with one of those singing "Billy Bass" plaques,* bring it in and sing along with the singing fish.

Practical Tips

- *Although we included this transition in the Large and Small Motor category, use it in the Imagination category if you like.*
- *Expand interest in this activity by making fishing poles out of paper towel tubes and string.*
- *Tape some small plastic or cardboard fish on the lines.*

*This popular item in gag gift shops a few years ago consists of a plaque with a mounted fish. When you push a button, the fish begins to move and sing a song.

Make-Over Madness

Objective
To develop fine motor skills by buttoning, zippering, and the like

Approximate Time
7–12 minutes

Ages
3–7

Required Materials
A large assortment of random clothing items and accessories
A large box

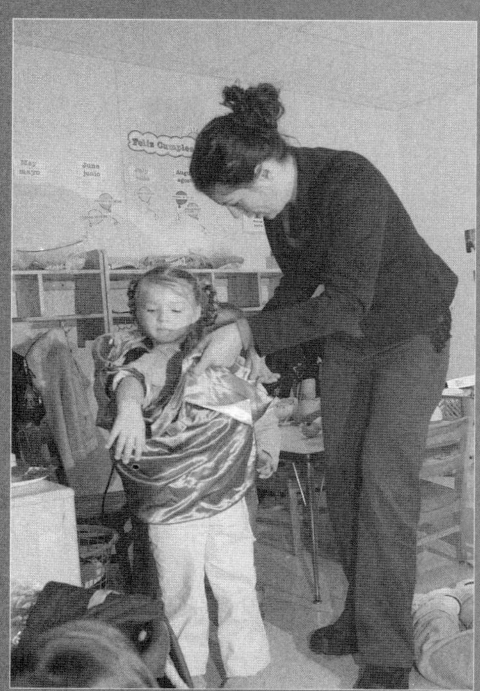

- Place clothing accessories in the giant box and set it out of the children's reach (the items should include a large assortment, such as plaid pants, Hawaiian print shirts, house slippers, high-heeled shoes, necklaces, wigs, hats, purses, sunglasses, etc.).
- Select a child to be your special volunteer supermodel (you will want to select a child who is somewhat confident in front of other children).
- As you slowly pull each individual item from the box, ask the children questions such as:
  - What is this?
  - Where do you wear it?
  - Should we have Jimmy wear it? (to which the children almost always respond with a nearly unanimous and loud "YEAH!").
- Have the model add each item (the goal is to make the clothing ensemble look as ridiculous as possible and to get the children to laugh).
- When you've gone through all the clothes (or run out of time), toss all the clothes back into the box.

(continues)

Make-Over Madness *(continued)*

Practical Tips

- *Use this transition as an opportunity for the children to practice small motor skills such as buttoning and zipping.*
- *With older children, consider using two bags (paper or plastic bags like the ones you get at the grocery store) and doing this as a relay.*

Super Spy Shoe Phone

Objective
To use large and small motor skills

Approximate Time
5–7 minutes

Ages
3–6

Required Materials
NONE

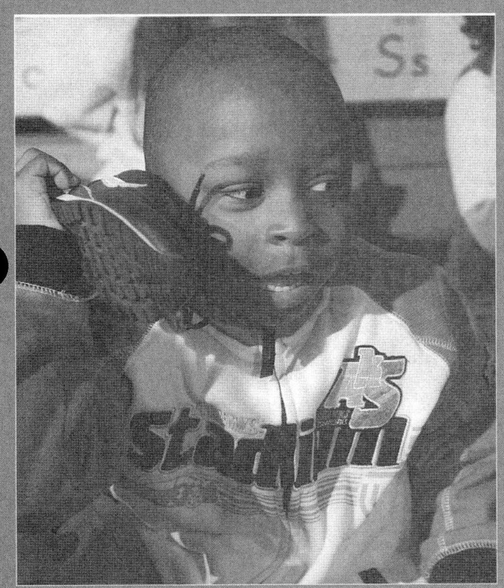

- Use this transition just before an activity that requires leaving the room, such as lunch, snack, going to the playground, or loading on the bus for a fieldtrip.
- Tell the children they will be leaving the room to go to your destination but you forgot to make reservations. You can't go without making reservations, so someone has to do this.
- Ask the children if any of them want to make reservations (probably, most of them will volunteer), and tell them you will do this together.
- Ask them how they would make reservations (they'll shout out a few things, and eventually someone will suggest calling).
- Once someone has suggested calling, act suddenly as if you've just had a terrific idea (you could even say, "I just had the most incredible idea!").
- Tell them you'll teach them how to use the top secret super spy shoe phone.
- Have them take a shoe off (then sniff it . . . or without the sniff part!).
- Using the shoe as a "phone," have them pretend to dial an imaginary number to reach the person you are pretending to call. Make ringing sounds with the children.

(continues)

Super Spy Shoe Phone *(continued)*

- Act as if you got the answering machine (mimic the voice on the answering machine, and say something like "Hi, we're not able to pick up the phone right now, so please leave a message and we'll try to call you back later." BEEP).
- Ask the children to leave a message. Whisper what you want them to say, and have them say it all together into their individual shoe phones ("Hi! This is Mrs. [Whatever's] class and we're getting ready to go to [wherever], okay? Thank you. 'Bye.") Then have the children hang up their shoe phones.
- Have the children put their shoes back on—which is great practice for them.
- Have them line up and go to snack or lunch or outside, or wherever you were intending to go.

Practical Tips

- *Reserve this activity for children who know how to tie their shoes.*
- *Use the transition at a time when you want everyone to take off their shoes anyway, such as naptime.*

Objective
To use large and small motor skills and recognize food by sight

Approximate Time
10–25 minutes

Ages
3–8

Required Materials
Apron and wig
A large mixing bowl
Utensils—spatula, large spoon, whisk
Several miscellaneous food items, condiments, and liquids (a great way to clean out the fridge!)

Have a Look at Cookin' with Patsy

- In advance, get a cooking apron and a crazy wig to bring to class.
- Before the activity, set out all of supplies on a small table or countertop (low enough so the children can see and reach what's on top of it).
- Have all the children sit on the floor at a good distance from the table.
- Take on the voice of a funny cooking character (this will make the activity more fun for you and the students—as well as any co-workers who happen by!). Tell the children you're going to be cooking up a nice casserole but you forgot the instructions. Tell them you will try to remember how to make the food but you might need a little help.
    - Hold up one of the items you've laid out on the table, and ask the children if you should put it in the casserole (they'll most likely vote yes).
    - Select someone to add the item to the mixing bowl.

- Repeat this with other children for all the ingredients (start with ingredients that might naturally go together, then slowly add bizarre ingredients to the mix).

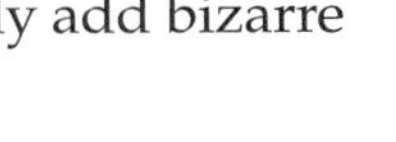

(continues)

Have a Look at Cookin' with Patsy *(continued)*

- When the children have finished adding all the ingredients, ask for volunteers to stir the casserole, and give the big spoon and the whisk to different volunteers to take turns.
- When the mysterious concoction is well mixed, show the students their disgusting creation (they'll probably respond with a resounding, "OOOOH . . . YUCK!").
- Ask if anyone wants to taste the casserole (you probably won't have many takers!).

Practical Tips

- *Use this activity when you want the children to practice small motor skills, such as stirring and mixing.*
- *Don't let the children taste the concoction. After all, it might make them sick!*

What's All the Racket?

Objective
To practice coordination and large and small motor skills

Approximate Time
7–12 minutes

Ages
3–8

Required Materials
Optional: Several toy musical instruments—tambourines, xylophones, drumsticks, etc.

- Select an easy-to-learn song for this activity, perhaps a song the children already know (such as the A-B-C song, "Quacky the Quack-a-Doodle Duck-a-Roo," and similar songs).
- Have all the children sit on the floor.
- Sing your pre-picked song a few times so the children get the hang of it.

- Then have them clap or pat a beat with their hands or on their knees (it can be as easy or as difficult as you want, depending on the children's ages).
- Sing the song to your original rhythmic beat.
- If you have the time and resources, hand out musical instruments and have the children tap out a beat with tambourines, xylophones, drumsticks, etc. (expect some noise-driven chaos, but the children will love it).
- Now sing your song to the rhythmic sounds the children produce.

(continues)

What's All the Racket? *(continued)*

Practical Tips

- *For this transition, get out that beginner band instrument you have tucked away.*
- *If you or someone you know plays a real instrument, ask him or her to join in. The children will enjoy the music that much more.*

Singing—With or Without Actions

The activities in this category are intended to:

- Expose children to music as an easy, go-anywhere transition.
- Use music as a background while the children are engaged in other activities.
- Enhance children's imagination through music.
- Expose children to various types of music—classical, classic rock, big band, jazz, the blues.
- Get the children to move and dance to the music—which also reinforces large and small motor skills.

SINGING

Put Your Finger on the Wall

Objective
To walk down a hall in an orderly fashion while also recognizing some body parts

Approximate Time
5–10 minutes

Ages
3–6

Required Materials
NONE

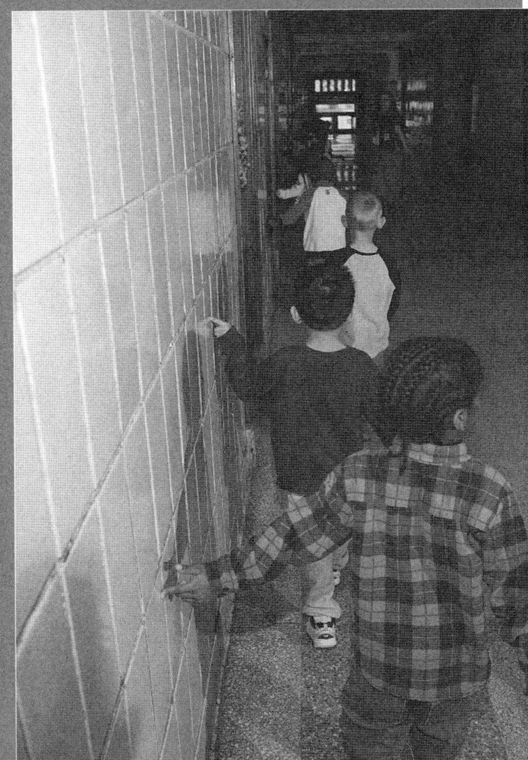

- Sing to the tune of "If You're Happy and You Know It":

  Put your finger on the wall, on the wall.

  Put your finger on the wall, on the wall.

  Put your finger on the wall, put your finger on the wall,

  Put your finger on the wall, on the wall.

- Have the children run a finger along the wall and sing as they walk. You'll be where you are going before you know it.

Practical Tips

- *As a variation, use the hand—or wrist or ear or elbow—instead of the finger. Don't use the nose or mouth, and make sure the children's hands are clean.*

SINGING

There Was a Wise Old King

OBJECTIVE
To sing, expend energy, and understand the concepts of UP and DOWN

APPROXIMATE TIME: 5–10 minutes

AGES: 3–7

REQUIRED MATERIALS
NONE

- Start a singing activity with this song, which has a simple, repetitive tune and simple words. If you can't come up with a tune to fit, do it as a chant.

  There was a wise old king
  Who had ten thousand men.
  He marched them up a hill and marched them down again.
  And when you're up, you're up.
  And when you're down, you're down.
  And when you're only halfway up, you're neither up nor down.

  - Have the children begin while they are sitting down.
  - When you come to "when you're up," have them stand up.
- When you come to "when you're down," have them sit down.

(continue

There Was a Wise Old King *(continued)*

- For "when you're only halfway up," have them hover between up and down.

Practical Tips

- *Use this song at varying tempos. Start out singing it really slowly, then get faster and faster each time you sing it.*
- *As another variation, go fast, then slow, and then fast again.*
- *Use the "when you're only halfway up" phrase to pause and have the children hanging in the middle.*

The Clean-Up Song

Objective
To pick up toys or the area

Approximate Time
5–10 minutes

Ages
3–6

Required Materials
NONE

- Sing the familiar tune that instructs the children to:

  Clean-up, clean, everybody, everywhere.
  Clean-up, clean, everybody do their share.

Practical Tips

- *Use this terrific repetitious activity every time you want the children to pick up.*

Keep in mind that children respond to structure and order. This activity will help the children stay focused and make clean-up time more fun for them

SINGING

The Hokey Pokey

Objective
To work out the wiggles, and also to recognize body parts

Approximate Time
5–10 minutes

Ages
3–10

Required Materials
NONE

- Demonstrate while you sing the familiar "Hokey Pokey":

  You put your right hand in, you take your right hand out,

  You put your right hand in, and you shake it all about.

  You do the hokey pokey and you turn yourself around.

  That's what it's all about.

- Repeat, changing the lyrics to:

  ...left hand

  ...right elbow, left elbow

  ...right foot, left foot

  ...right leg, left leg

  ...right shoulder, left shoulder

  ...head...chin...tongue

  ...belly...bottom

  ...whole self

Practical Tips

- *Think up as many things as you can to hokey pokey with. Basically, if you've got it and it's presentable, it can hokey pokey!*
- *Have the children think up some parts, too.*

The Hand-Washing Song

Objective
To learn how wash the hands for the appropriate length of time

Approximate Time
5–10 minutes

Ages
3–6

Required Materials
NONE

- Sing with the children to the tune of "This Is the Way We..."

  This is the way we wash our hands, wash our hands, wash our hands.

  This is the way we wash our hands, every day.

  Soap and water, rub, rub, rub; rub, rub, rub; rub, rub, rub.

  Soap and water rub, rub, rub. Then you dry.

Practical Tips

- *Use this activity every time the children wash up. The song is just long enough to ensure proper sanitation.*
- *Introduce the activity when the children are very young, and wash your hands with them.*
- *Make sure they scrub the nails, palms, wrists, and each finger.*

SINGING

If We All Pick Up Toys

Objective
To pick up toys along with the teacher

Approximate Time
5–10 minutes

Ages
3–6

Required Materials
NONE

- Sing to the tune of "If We All Pull Together":

  If we all pick-up toys, pick-up toys, pick-up toys,

  If we all pick-up toys, how happy we'll be.

  Then your toys are picked-up and my toys are picked-up.

  If we all pick-up toys, how happy we'll be.

Practical Tips

- *Emphasize sharing in the clean-up time, not just during playtime.*

There Was a Child Who Had a Name

OBJECTIVE
To learn to spell their name

APPROXIMATE TIME
5–10 minutes

AGES
3–6

REQUIRED MATERIALS
NONE

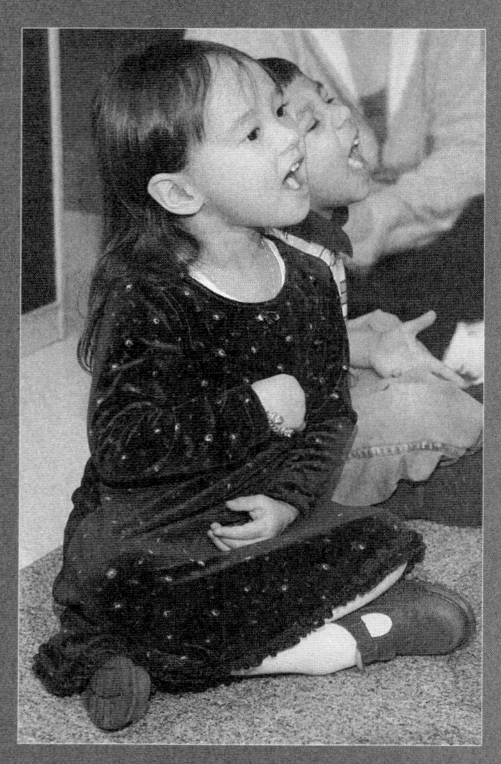

- Sing to the tune of "There Was a Farmer":

  There was a teacher who had a name,
  Mrs. Smith was her name-O.

  S M I T H, S M I T H, S M I T H. Mrs. Smith
  was her name-O.

  There was a boy who had a name, and
  Andrew was his name-O.

  A N D R E W, A N D R E W, A N D R E W. And
  Andrew was his name-O.

  There was a girl who had a name, and Juliet
  was her name-O.

  J U L I E T, J U L I E T, J U L I E T. And Juliet
  was her name-O.

- Sing until you have sung all the students' names. It doesn't matter if the letters fit into the tune exactly. Just keep going.

Practical Tips

- *Emphasize the positive individual attention that each child likes.*
- *Use this as an activity rather than a transition, in which the children learn to spell their own name and the names of their classmates as well.*

Where Is Thumbkin?

OBJECTIVE
To enhance small motor dexterity and learn about the hands

APPROXIMATE TIME
5–10 minutes

AGES
3–5

REQUIRED MATERIALS
NONE

- In this finger play, begin with one hand behind your back and the other hand with the thumb moving as if the thumb were singing.
- Sing to the tune of "Frère Jacques" ("Are You Sleeping"):

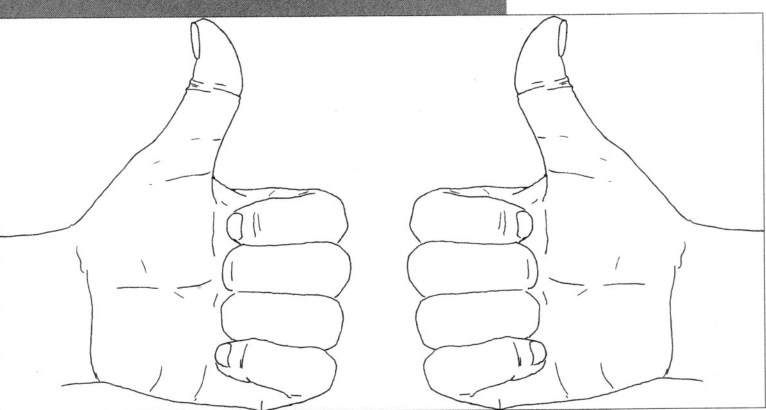

Where is Thumbkin, where is Thumbkin?

(Use the thumb on the other hand to answer) Here I am, here I am.

How are you today, sir?

Very fine, oh thank you.

Run away (the second hand behind your back as you sing)

Run away (the first hand behind your back)

- Go through the other fingers while you sing:

  Where is Pointer?

  Where is Tall Man?

  Where is Ring Man?

  Where is Pinky?

  And where's the family? (the whole hand)

(continues)

SINGING

Where Is Thumbkin? *(continued)*

Practical Tips

- *Vary this song from soft to loud. Have the children sing the entire song in a normal tone, then sing the song a second time really loud through each verse. End with a very soft version, getting softer and softer as you sing each verse (almost whispering as you end).*
- *Use this as a transition to help children get the wiggles out and then quiet down.*

SINGING

The Quiet-Time Song

Objective
To calm down before rest time

Approximate Time
5–10 minutes

Ages
3–4

Required Materials
NONE

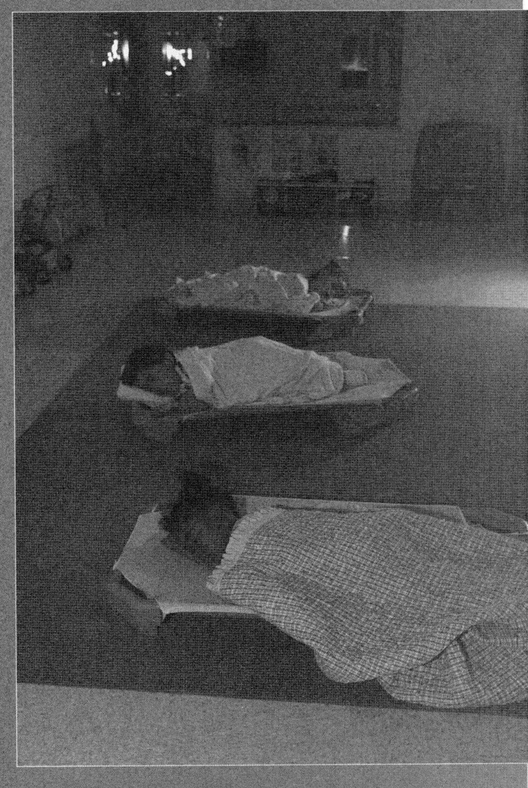

- Sing to the tune of "Brahm's Lullaby":

  It is now quiet time, it is time to slow down.

  All the toys are put away. Everyone has stopped their play.

  Now lie down, on your bed [mat][cot], and pull your blanket to your head.

  It is now quiet time. Quiet time is all that's said.

- Repeat, singing in a whisper this time.

Practical Tips

- *Develop a routine through repetition in the daily schedule.*
- *As a variation, have all the children try to get on their cot, mat, or bed by the time you whisper the song the first time through.*

Radio Sing-Along

Objective
To develop an appreciation for music

Approximate Time	**Ages**
5–10 minutes	3–6

Required Materials
A radio or tape/CD player and appropriate music

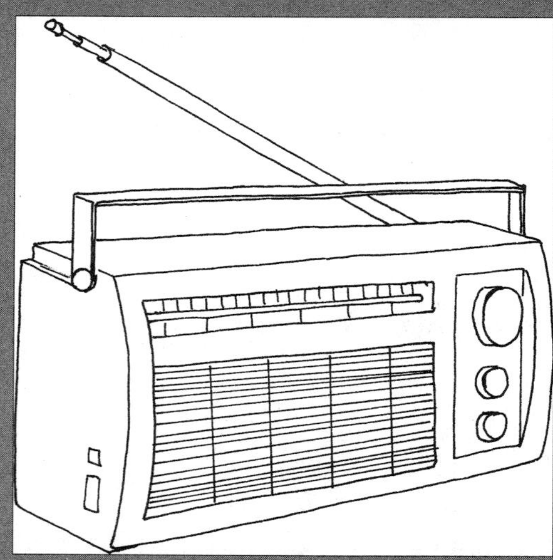

- Check out radio stations or CDs or tapes for different types of music—jazz, big band, classic rock, bluegrass, children's music. Make sure that the songs have understandable lyrics and that they are appropriate to the age group.
- When you come to a time in the day when you need a break from your routine or a transition, announce, "It's radio sing-along time!"
- Begin to play the music and sing along with it.
- Leading the way, encourage the children to sing, too.
- Dance around the room while pretending to have a microphone, or play an "air guitar" or "air drums." Encourage the children to join with you.
- When each song has ended, clap and cheer for your singers and players.

Practical Tips

- *Don't think you need a "music teacher" to have "music class!" It doesn't matter if you can carry a tune. All you need is to have the music—and to dispense with your fear of singing. The children won't care. They just love to sing.*
- *Instead of limiting this activity to transition times, make it a regularly scheduled activity that you call "Music Class" or "Music Hour."*

The Circle-Time Song

Objective
To participate in a musical circle time

Approximate Time
5–10 minutes

Ages
3–6

Required Materials
NONE

SINGING

- Sing to the tune of "Jingle Bells":

  Circle time, circle time. It is circle time.
  Oh what fun it is to join the class in circle time.
  Circle time, circle time. It is circle time.
  Come now, won't you join me as we sit in circle time?

- Lead the children around a taped circle on the floor as you sing.

(continues)

The Circle-Time Song *(continued)*

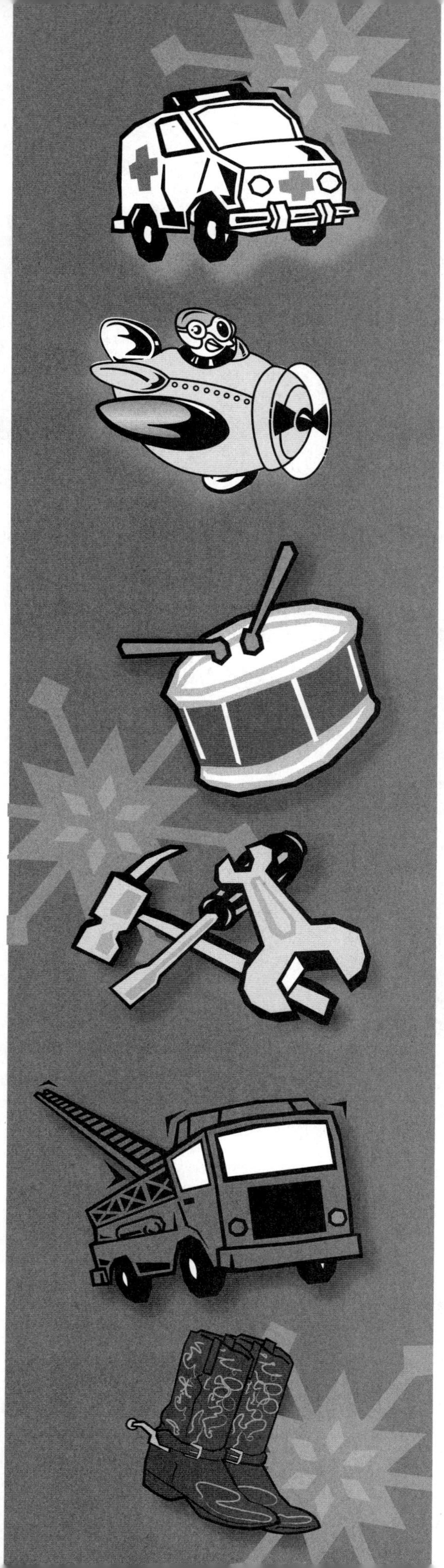

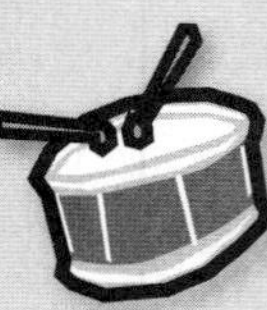

Practical Tips

- *Use songs like this one for transitions and to introduce new activities so the children will come to anticipate what is to follow. When they associate a certain song with a part of the daily routine, they will become more excited about changing activities.*
- *For children who have difficulty with change, use songs to create that mental link of familiarity that will make it seem like they aren't changing activities at all.*
- *For children who like change, use the familiar song as an exciting bridge to something new.*

Our Class Has Many Children

Objective
To build math concepts and counting skills

Approximate Time
5–10 minutes

Ages
3–6

Required Materials
NONE

- Sing to the tune of "One Little, Two Little, Three Little Indians":

  Our class has many children, our class has many children.

  Our class has many children. How many children here?

  One little, two little, three little children. Four little, five little, six little children.

  Seven little, eight little, nine little children. Ten little children here.

  Eleven little, twelve little, thirteen little children.

  Fourteen little, fifteen little, sixteen little children.

  Seventeen little, eighteen little, nineteen little children. Twenty little children here.

- When you reach the total of children in your group, end with [number] little children here.

(continues)

SINGING

Our Class Has Many Children *(continued)*

Practical Tips

- *Make this transition a part of the daily roll call routine. It will involve the children in something you should be doing constantly during the day: counting the children, being aware of the number present at any given time, and ensuring that they are all present and accounted for.*

Quiet Down/Crowd Control

The activities in this category are intended to:

- Get the children to quiet down when desired.
- Allow the children to be loud for a few minutes at times.
- Be a follow-up to other types of transitions.
- Gain the children's attention and get them to calm down, slow down, and quiet down.
- Be as simple as a series of hand claps for which children are taught to listen.

Talking Box

OBJECTIVE
To enhance descriptive skills

APPROXIMATE TIME
7–12 minutes

AGES
3–5

REQUIRED MATERIALS
Speaker phone, intercom, walky-talky, or similar device

QUIET DOWN

- Have the children sit on the floor.
- Tell them we have a new "friend" in our class who is different from most of their other friends. His name is Sammy Speaker Phone (or Delores Intercom, or whatever name you want to use).
- Tell them that this friend has no eyes, so he or she can't see them, but he or she can hear them and they will be able to talk back and forth with their new friend.

- Have someone else on the other end ready to participate.
- Calling the speaker phone by the name you have chosen, say "hello."
- The speaker phone will answer: "Hello, boys and girls and [Mrs. Johnson]. I'm very glad to be here with your class today."
- Carry on a conversation with the device (the children will laugh even if they think they know who the voice is).

(continues)

Talking Box *(continued)*

Practical Tips

- *Use this activity to pique the children's imagination. They are intrigued by things they haven't yet experienced.*
- *Have the children describe something in the room to the "voice" in the box. This will hone their observation and descriptive skills and add another dimension to the game. Have the person on the other end respond by asking questions for the children to add to the description.*

The Quiet Game

Objective
To quiet down

Approximate Time
2–5 minutes

Ages
3–4

Required Materials
NONE

- Tell the children: "Let's see who can be the most quiet. I will count to three, and when I say 'go,' everyone will be quiet. The first one to talk loses that round of the game."
- Say, "Ready: 1 . . . 2 . . . 3 . . . Go!"
- After that, say, "Okay, Let's try it again."

Practical Tips

- *Don't overuse or overextend this activity, as children are not geared to be quiet all the time. Use it once in a while to get them to quiet down so you can go on to something else.*
- *Use this activity within 2–5 minutes maximum.*

I'm Looking for a Volunteer Who . . .

Objective
To sit quietly in preparation for a new activity

Approximate Time
5–10 minutes

Ages
3–6

Required Materials
NONE

- Use this activity as a transition to another activity that requires a helper (someone to pass out the napkins for snack, be the line leader, pick up crayons, or whatever the children volunteer to do).
- Say, "I'm looking for a volunteer who is sitting quietly at the table, with hands folded, finished coloring, who . . ." (add any conditions you like).
- End by picking someone as a volunteer.

Practical Tips

- *Use this activity anywhere, anytime. Just change the criteria.*

I Spy with My Little Eye

Objective
To focus on calming down and to enhance recognition skills

Approximate Time
5–10 minutes

Ages
3–7

Required Materials
NONE

- In this old favorite, designate someone to be the "spy."
- Have the "spy" pick something in plain sight of everyone in the group and describe it: "I spy with my little eye . . . something that is small and round and long. It is on the table, and it is used to write with."
  - Ask everyone to guess (such as "a pencil").

Practical Tips

- *Begin this activity with yourself as the "spy," and after several rounds have children take turns being the "spy." Designate the one who makes the first correct guess to be the next "spy."*

QUIET DOWN

Let's Sneak Up on the Other Class

Objective
To walk quietly as a group

Approximate Time
5–10 minutes

Ages
3–6

Required Materials
NONE

- Use this activity when you are trying to move a group of children from one place to another.
- Tell them they are going to sneak all the way to the playground (or wherever) without anyone hearing them.
  - Put on your "sneaky tennis shoes" and zip your "shssh guard" over your lips.
  - Lead the children in the "tiptoe creep."
  - Take turns slinking around corners.
  - After you get to where you are going, make a big deal about how sneaky and quiet the children were.

Practical Tips

- *Use your imagination to make this a fun activity while accomplishing your goal of quietly going from one place to another. It demonstrates how you can make a game out of everyday activities.*

25

Who's in the Closet?

Objective
To become calm and quiet

Approximate Time	**Ages**
2–10 minutes	3–6

Required Materials
A closet in the room
A puppet or animal (live or stuffed) or a person

- While the children are out of the room or preoccupied, hide a stuffed animal, puppet, or person in the closet.
- When you are ready for the transitional activity, act as if you are hearing noises.

- Ask the children to be quiet so you can figure out what it is and where it is coming from.
- Indicate that there's something in the closet, and tell all the children it must be a "special friend."
- Have the children sit up straight and get really quiet so their shy friend will come out and visit. You could even get the children to count to three and yell, "Come out and play!" (or something to that effect) a few times to try to coax their shy friend to visit.
- Open the closet door wide and bring out the hidden guest.

(continues)

Who's in the Closet? *(continued)*

- Have all the children say "hi" and tell their visitor what they've been doing that day.
- When time is up, have the children say goodbye to their visitor and ask the guest to go back "home" (to the closet).

Practical Tips

- *Do this activity again and again, as children don't tire of suspense and like to be surprised—but change the "friend" each time.*
- *Use your own imagination and make "friends" out of everyday things such as a soccer ball with eyes, or a sock puppet. You can even make a hamburger box talk!*

Questions About a Missing Person

OBJECTIVE
To enhance observation skills

APPROXIMATE TIME
3–10 minutes

AGES
3–8

REQUIRED MATERIALS
NONE

QUIET DOWN

- Remove a person from the room (may be one of the children or another teacher). It doesn't matter that the children know who has left the group.
- Begin asking questions about the person who is now absent, for example:
  - Was he wearing a T-shirt or a button-up shirt?
  - What kind of pants, slacks, or shorts was she wearing?
  - Was he wearing glasses?
  - What kind of shoes was she wearing?
  - What color is his hair?
  - Was there anything different about her today?
  - What picture was on his T-shirt?
  - Was she wearing a belt?
- After asking all the questions, have the children tell you anything else they noticed about that person.
- When you are finished, bring the person back into the room and see how close the children were in their answers.

(continues)

Questions About a Missing Person *(continued)*

Practical Tips

- *Use this activity when you or your teaching assistant have to leave the room for a minute or two.*
- *If the missing person is a teacher, observe how much attention the children actually pay to the teacher's appearance and clothing each day!*

Everybody Point!

QUIET DOWN

OBJECTIVE
To gain quick recognition and listening skills

APPROXIMATE TIME
5–12 minutes

AGES
3–8

REQUIRED MATERIALS
NONE

- Have the children sit down as a group, and tell them they are going to play the game "Everybody Point!"
- State the simple rules to the game: No one can speak or make a noise. They can communicate only by pointing.

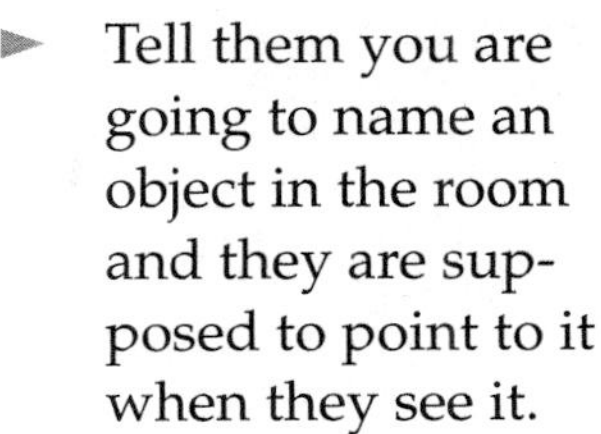

- Tell them you are going to name an object in the room and they are supposed to point to it when they see it.

- Begin to name things in the room that are easy to find: the ceiling, the door to the bathroom, the chalkboard. . . .
- When they point to it, acknowledge that they are correct. Do not go on to another object until everyone is pointing to the object you just named.
- Now begin to name more difficult things: brown velcro shoes on one of the children, the ceiling tile with the brown stain on it. . . .

(continues)

QUIET DOWN

Everybody Point! *(continued)*

- After playing several rounds, have one or two of the children name objects.

Practical Tips

- *Use this game to reinforce the new environment of very young children as they learn the names of things around them.*

Make-Believe Story Land

OBJECTIVE
To enhance creativity, listening skills, and memory skills

APPROXIMATE TIME	**AGES**
7–20 minutes	3–10

REQUIRED MATERIALS
None (Optional: a dry-erase board and markers or chalk and chalkboard)

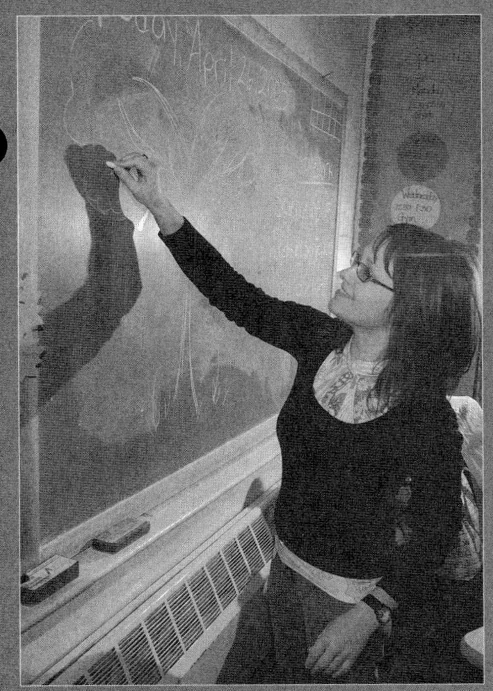

- Have the children sit in a group.
- Tell them that they are going to help you make up a story, and that you have a special magic drawing board that will help.
- Begin to draw something—anything—and ask the children what it is.
- As they identify what you are drawing, follow their lead and try to make it look like what they are describing. (If they say, for example, "That's a banana-headed monkey," go with what they say.)
- Ask them leading questions such as:
  - Who are our two characters here?
  - What are they doing today?
- As you continue, ask questions to encourage them to keep developing the story ("Where are they going?" "Who are they going to see?") It doesn't matter if the story makes little sense. Keep them imagining and interested.
- When their interest seems to fade, start a different story or move on to the next activity.

(continues)

Make-Believe Story Land *(continued)*

Practical Tips

- *Encourage children's vivid imagination through this activity.*
- *Validate the children's ideas and imaginative expression, even if their ideas are preposterous.*

Let's Write (or Tell) a Story

Objective
To enhance teamwork and imagination

Approximate Time
5–10 minutes

Ages
3–12

Required Materials
Paper and pencils

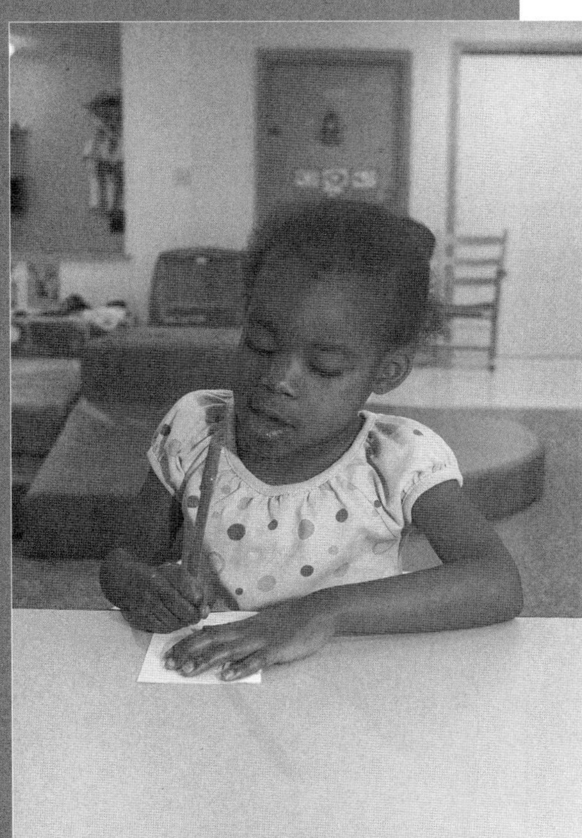

QUIET DOWN

- Tell the children that they are going to finish a story and that you are going to read the start to the story.
- If the children are old enough to write, hand out pieces of paper. (If not, see the Practical Tips.)
  - Read a starter phrase such as, "It was a dark and stormy night . . ." or "Then the three boys looked back at . . ." or "Nobody seemed to notice when I. . . ."
  - Have the children take turns expanding on the story with a sentence or two. If the group is large, circulate more than one story at a time.
  - Allow enough time for the children to write down the additions to the story.
  - When everyone is finished writing, read the story aloud.

(continues)

Let's Write (or Tell) a Story *(continued)*

Practical Tips

- *For younger children, work together to tell a story instead of writing it down. Do this by asking the children to keep adding something. If they get stumped, help them out or start a different story.*
- *In this activity, be lenient. The story doesn't have to make sense.*

Mouth Full of Bubbles

Objective
To become quiet for a minute or two

Approximate Time
5–10 minutes

Ages
3–6

Required Materials
NONE

QUIET DOWN

- Let the children know that it is time to quiet down.
- Ask them to make believe they have a mouthful of good-tasting bubbles

- Tell them that if their mouth were full of bubbles, their cheeks would be puffed out and they wouldn't be able to talk or even open their mouth because they would lose their bubbles (show them how their cheeks would look).
- Have them blow their mouth full of air (imaginary bubbles) until their cheeks fill out.
- Praise them for having such a big mouth full of bubbles.

(continues)

QUIET DOWN

Mouth Full of Bubbles *(continued)*

Practical Tips

- *Use this activity as one of your best standbys to get the group to quiet down.*
- *As with many other activities, alternate this one with other activities to keep the children from getting bored.*

Soldiers on Parade

Objective
To learn to work together as a group

Approximate Time
5–10 minutes

Ages
3–8

Required Materials
NONE

- Tell the children that they are group of top-notch soldiers on a secret mission and that before they can go on this important and highly secret mission, they must undergo training.
- Get them to walk and talk like soldiers (march in place at attention; salute someone who is walking by; come to attention when you say "ATTENTION," do the "Army crawl," or practice sliding around corners).

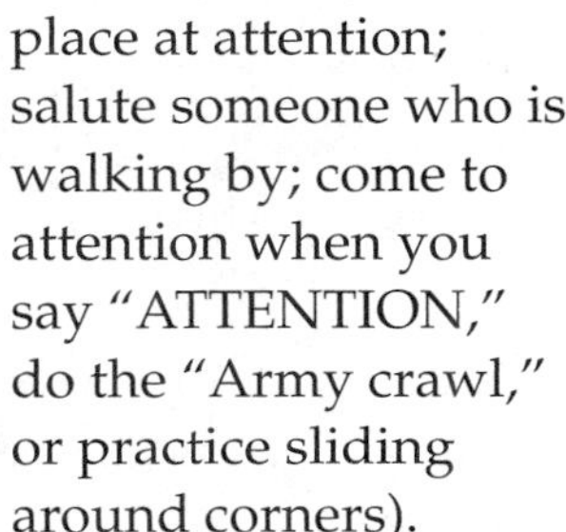

- Create a make-believe mission and call it something like "Capture the Flag"(capture cookies for snacks, or find the missing basketballs for the playground).
- Make sure the children understand that to be successful in this mission, they must work together as a group, stay together, and be quiet.

(continues)

Soldiers on Parade *(continued)*

Practical Tips

- *Use this activity when you want to combine movement with the transition.*
- *Put your innovative nature into action to make an adventure out of a mundane activity. Your students will be on the edge of their seats wondering what you'll think of next!*

Make-Believe Chewing Gum

OBJECTIVE
To quiet down

APPROXIMATE TIME
5–10 minutes

AGES
3–8

REQUIRED MATERIALS
NONE

- Use this activity when you want a variation on Mouth Full of Bubbles (Activity 30)—which is similar except that this one uses make-believe chewing gum.
- Have everyone take an imaginary piece of invisible, make-believe chewing gum and begin to chew. They can go through the whole imaginary exercise of opening the package, taking out a stick of gum, unwrapping it, throwing away the wrapping paper, and putting it in their mouth.
- Remind them that polite people chew with their mouth closed.

(continues)

QUIET DOWN

Make-Believe Chewing Gum *(continued)*

Practical Tips

- *Compliment the children who are "chewing" the most quietly. Children like to think they are doing something right or good.*
- *Even if you usually don't want children to blow and pop their gum, turn this activity into a slightly noisier version—if you make clear that they may do this only when you say so. You decide!*

QUIET DOWN

Objective
To learn about the differences in sounds

Approximate Time
5–10 minutes

Ages
3–6

Required Materials
NONE

What Sound Does the Wind Make?

- Ask the children to sit on the floor as a group.
- Begin by talking loud, then softer . . . and softer: "**Everyone come** over here and sit down." Let's sit down really quietly. . . . Now think really hard. What sound does the wind make?"

- Give the children a chance to answer.
- "Sometimes the wind is **loud!**" (Start blowing loudly.) "And sometimes the wind is really quiet."
- "Let's pretend we are **loud wind.**" (Encourage everyone be loud wind, and you join in.)
- (whispering) "Let's pretend we are really quiet wind." (Encourage everyone to sound like really soft wind).
- (whispering very quietly) "Shh—can you hear that? Can you hear the silence?"

(continues)

QUIET DOWN

What Sound Does the Wind Make? *(continued)*

Practical Tips

- *Use this activity to introduce concepts of weather in keeping with the age level.*
- *If children have a fear of strong winds, use this activity to dispel the fears.*

Recognition/Memory

The activities in this category are intended to:

- Expand children's knowledge, memory, and recognition of objects or concepts.
- Be used especially with young children between ages three and five.
- Be adapted for children in middle school in some cases.

34

Quiet or Loud

OBJECTIVE
To understand concepts of quiet and loud

APPROXIMATE TIME
2–10 minutes

AGES
3–10

REQUIRED MATERIALS
NONE

- Use this activity to quiet the children when you need to tell them something—for example, "We need to clean up now" or "We're getting ready to do. . . . " Children are used to being shhhhhhed, and this gives it a fun twist.
- Start by having them be very loud, because it points out the contrast between loud and soft. Say, "I want everyone to be as loud as you can. Come on, everyone—be LOUD!" All the children should scream back at you as loud as they can.

- Then tell them, "Now I want you all to be as quiet as you can." Have them keep getting quieter and quieter until they are completely silent.
- Go back and forth several times between loud and quiet: "Everybody be loud!" then "Everybody be quiet." (For younger children, you might have to explain that you are going to do this, but with older children you probably can jump right in.)
- After doing this several times, tell them the information you want them to know.
- Then go back and do the loud and quiet part again.

(continues)

Quiet or Loud *(continued)*

Practical Tips

- *Use this versatile activity inside or outside, during another activity, or for a transition.*
- *Consider this activity as a game, a fun alternative to nagging children to be quiet.*

Up or Down

Objective
To understand the concepts of "up" and "down"

Approximate Time
2–5 minutes

Ages
3–8

Required Materials
NONE

- Have the children sit on the floor in one location, and tell them you are going to play a game called "Up or Down."
- Give a few examples so they will know what you expect. First ask, "Where's the ceiling?" Point up and say, "It's up!" Then, "Where's the floor?" Point down and have the children say "down."
- Now look around the room and name objects. Pick items that are clearly either up or down, and have the children respond "up" or "down."
- Have all the children shout out the answer all together, or have them raise their hand to be called on to answer (this also reinforces their learning to sit quietly and listen).

Practical Tips

- *With older children, ask more abstract questions: "Where do birds fly? Where do you plant flowers? How do we grow?"*
- *With older children and more difficult up or down items, make this a game to see how fast they can answer.*
- *Have the children stand and sit slowly, then start going faster. This will help release their energy.*
- *Expand the activity by having the children use their motor skills: crouch down and stand up, put their hands, feet, or head up and down, and so forth.*

MEMORY

In or Out

Objective
To understand the concepts of "in" and "out"

Approximate Time
10–20 minutes

Ages
3–5

Required Materials
Masking tape

- Outline a large square on the floor with masking tape.
- Tell the children, "We're going to discuss the difference between "in" and "out." Say, for example, "These words are opposites, words that mean the reverse, like hot and cold."

- Call the children's attention to the outline of the square on the floor.
- Step into the square and ask, "Who would like to get in the box with me?" (I'll bet they all will!)
- When they step inside, say, "Billy is IN the box. . . . Oh, now Julie is IN the box. . . . We're all IN the box."
- Now say, "Let's all get OUT of the box." Then jump out of the box and make a big deal about being out of the box.
- When everyone is out of the box, say, "Let's get back IN the box!" Then get back out.
- Keep alternating in and out while getting quicker and quicker.

(contin

In or Out *(continued)*

Practical Tips

- *Keep the taped box around for a few days and use it for a transition by saying, "When you get your area all picked up, get in the box" or "When you're ready to go to lunch, get in the box."*
- *Give your box a name, such as the "In and Out Box" or "Fred the box."*
- *Get a copy of Farrel and Farrel's* People in the Box *and play it while you are doing the activity.*

MEMORY

MEMORY

Objective
To understand the difference between sitting down and standing up

Approximate Time	**Ages**
5–15 minutes	3–6

Required Materials
NONE

Ring Around the Rosie

- Teach the children how to make a circle while holding hands and how to go around in a circle as a group.
- Chant or sing:

  Ring around the rosie,
  A pocket full of posies.
  Ashes, ashes,
  We all fall down.

- Instruct the children to change the words to "sit down" instead of "fall down."
- Go through the motions, and then have them sit down at the end.
- Tell them that to "win" at this part of game, they have to be sitting quietly at the end of the chant (or song), with their hands folded nicely in their lap.
- As they get quiet, say something like, "Oh, yes, I see that Jonah is sitting down like he's supposed to . . . and so is Hannah. Oh yes, Noah, you're doing it right, too."
- Tell the children that they are going to whisper-chant (or sing) it again, but instead of holding hands and going around in a circle, they are going to sit still and move only their head in a circle.

(continue

Ring Around the Rosie *(continued)*

- Lead the children in the song (chant), and when you come to the part "and we all . . .," say "and we all stand-up" and stand to your feet.
- Tell them that to "win" at this part of the game, they must stand up straight with their hands at their sides like soldiers standing at attention.
- Praise each child when he or she follows the instruction.
- After practicing this exercise several times, use it to get the children to sit down, such as at circle time or when you want them to sit in chairs at tables. Have them "ring around" by themselves, and when they come to the "sit down" part, they have to be in the circle or in their chairs.

Practical Tips

- *Use the "stand up" part of the activity to get the children in a line or moving from the circle time or chairs to another activity.*

MEMORY

38

What Did You Do This Past Weekend?

Objective
To increase memory and listening skills

Approximate Time
10–20 minutes

Ages
3–12

Required Materials
NONE

MEMORY

- Have the children sit on the floor in a semi-circle.
- Tell them you were looking forward to coming back to school on Monday because you couldn't wait to hear about the exciting adventures they had over the weekend; you know they have a lot of exciting stories and they will be telling about it.

- Before you start, encourage the children to practice their listening skills so the others will listen to them when it is their turn.
- Give each child personal attention by going around the room and choosing the children one by one to tell about their weekend. Ask each child in turn, "What did you do this weekend?" (The younger children tend to embellish a little, but that's okay—they want to sound exciting.)

(continued)

What Did You Do This Past Weekend? *(continued)*

- As each child finishes, ask the others to make him or her feel special by clapping and cheering.

Practical Tips

- *Use this activity particularly to teach and practice listening. No matter how old you are, you want others to listen to what you have to say. People get a sense of worth from receiving undivided attention without interruptions or corrections.*
- *As an alternative, use this activity on a Friday to get the children excited about their weekend. Ask them what kind of adventures they think they will have this weekend. Have them tell about the fun things they hope to do before Monday.*
- *Incorporate this activity when the children are working at their desks doing an art project or coloring, to help keep them from getting bored.*

MEMORY

What Do You Want for Christmas? (or Your Next Birthday)

OBJECTIVE
To further recognition and memory skills, as well as to increase imagination

APPROXIMATE TIME
10–20 minutes

AGES
3–12

REQUIRED MATERIALS
NONE

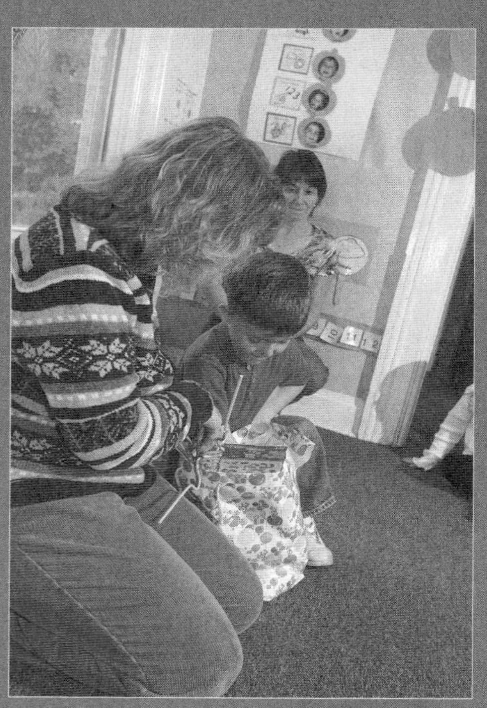

Note: Not all children and families celebrate Christmas or birthdays. Use this activity at your discretion. It might be a good opportunity to help all the children learn something about each other and about different celebrations.

- Use this activity as an opportunity to let kids be kids and to share their dreams.
- Remind the children as a group that Christmas (or their birthday) is coming, even if it is a long way off.
- Ask each child if he or she could receive anything at all for Christmas (or birthday), no matter what the cost, what would it be, and why? The answers will reveal a piece of each child's personality.
- Finally, take your turn and tell the children what you would like as a gift, and why.

(continue

What Do You Want for Christmas? (or Your Next Birthday) *(continued)*

Practical Tips

- *Use this activity to give each child a moment of personal attention that will boost his or her self-esteem.*

  Don't be reluctant to use this activity if the holiday isn't close at hand. It's always good to encourage children to dream and wish.

- *Use this activity for any celebration that reflects the culture of the group.*

MEMORY

Where Do You Want To Go on Vacation?

Objective
To use recall and memory as a foundation for imagination

Approximate Time	**Ages**
10–20 minutes	3–12

Required Materials
NONE

- Assemble the children and ask them who likes to go on vacation (the children may be nearly unanimous in their hearty reply!).
- Tell them you are planning a vacation and are trying to figure out where to go.

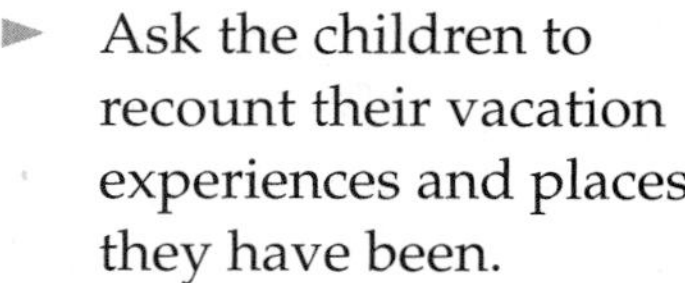

- Ask the children to recount their vacation experiences and places they have been.

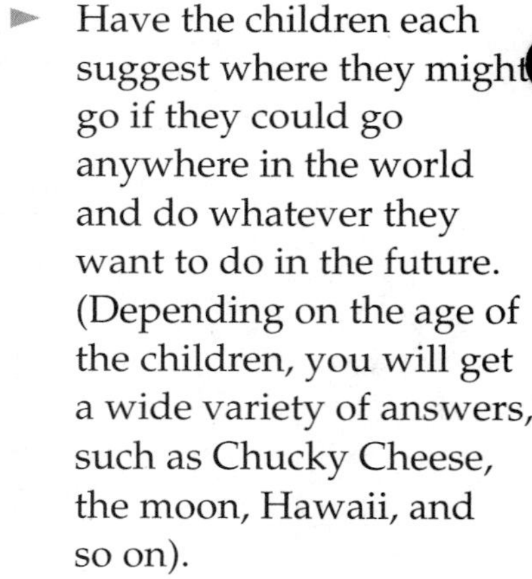

- Have the children each suggest where they might go if they could go anywhere in the world and do whatever they want to do in the future. (Depending on the age of the children, you will get a wide variety of answers, such as Chucky Cheese, the moon, Hawaii, and so on).
- Ask each child why he or she would want to go there, and give each child an opportunity to expand on the reasons.

(continued)

Where Do You Want To Go on Vacation? *(continued)*

Practical Tips

- *Encourage the children to use their memory in telling details about where they have gone on vacation.*
- *Keep in mind that there are no wrong answers about where the children would want to go. Encourage their imagination.*

Line Up by Color

OBJECTIVE
To make a transition to go somewhere by getting into a line, and at the same time increase color recognition skills

APPROXIMATE TIME
5–15 minutes

AGES
3–10

REQUIRED MATERIALS
NONE

- Take a creative approach to the sometimes rowdy line-up time by having the children line up by color (this works especially well with younger children who are just learning their colors).
- Start by saying, "Whoever is wearing something red (or whatever color you choose) can line up."
- Go through the other colors until all the children are lined up.

- If you have enough time, elaborate by being more specific (for example, "Whoever is wearing red shoes can get in line").
- If you have the luxury of having an extra teacher or an aide, have him or her cover his or her eyes and call out colors (this will keep any children from feeling singled out).

Practical Tips

- *Use this activity as a way for the children to heighten awareness of those around them as they look for the colors.*
- *Use this transition as an activity, rather than a transition, to teach colors to younger children.*

MEMORY

Line Up by Clothing

Objective
To increase knowledge and recognition of shapes, textures, colors, and similar concepts

Approximate Time	**Ages**
5–15 minutes	3–10

Required Materials
Just children wearing clothes!

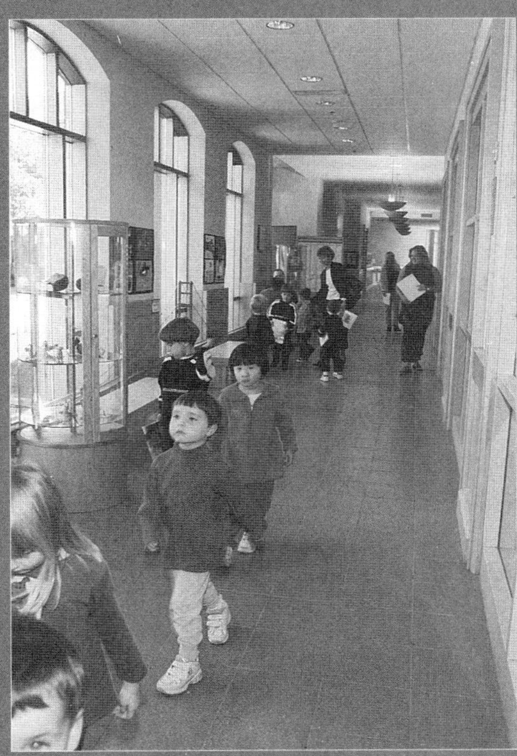

- Use this activity as a follow-up to Activity 41, or one requiring more advanced skills (it requires the children to pay closer attention).
- Tell the children it is time to line up but they are going to have to put on their "thinking caps."
- Call out different categories: "Anyone with short hair line up. . . . Anyone with long hair line up. . . . Those with green eyes line up. . . ." You can announce those with painted fingernails, those wearing jeans, shorts, and so on (the options are innumerable, limited only by your own creativity).
- Make this activity as lengthy or as brief as you like.
- If you have more time, stipulate to older children that they may line up if they can find the person with "white shoes" (or whatever) to line up with them. This will encourage children to work together and to mix with children with whom they do not usually interact.

Practical Tips

- *Don't go for only the easy and obvious. Look for small details about the children and what they are wearing.*
- *Suggest specific combinations such as, "If you're wearing white tennis shoes, find someone with a yellow shirt to line up with."*

MEMORY

43

Line Up if You Can Tell Me Something

Objective
To increase recognition and memory as well as listening skills

Approximate Time
5–15 minutes

Ages
3–10

Required Materials
NONE

MEMORY

- With this transition, check to see how well the children have been listening to what you have taught throughout the day, and how well they have learned.

- Tell the children they are going to line up but they must answer one trivia question first.
- Say that you will call on children who are sitting quietly with only one arm raised.
- Select your questions depending on the age level and what you have been teaching during the past day, week, or month.
- Ask each child a different question. For example, if you had been teaching about animals, a sample question might be: What animal has orange and black stripes with big teeth and lives in the jungle?
- When a child answers correctly, give him or her the go-ahead to line up.
- Remind the children to behave while they are in line, and tell them they might have to sit down and answer another question before they will get the chance to line up again.

(continue

Line Up if You Can Tell Me Something *(continued)*

- If the children are older, ask more advanced questions to fit the learning content, and ask some tricky questions to make them think harder.

Practical Tips

- *Use this activity as a tried-and-true motivational tool to get your students to listen and pay attention throughout the day.*
- *Don't let the questions drag on too long or the children already in line will become bored.*

MEMORY

44

MEMORY

Animal High-Dive Competition

Objective
To identify animals by sound and characteristics

Approximate Time
7–15 minutes

Ages
3–5

Required Materials
Large transparent tub of water
Several plastic animals
Paper bag
Paper towels

- Place the tub of water out of the children's reach.
- Take the collection of animals you've concealed in the paper bag, and position yourself directly above the tub of water.
- Tell the children you've captured a whole bunch of little animals and they're inside the bag.
- Take out one animal at a time and ask the children to say the name of the animal, what color(s) it is, and to mimic the sound each animal makes.
- After each animal has been named and described, ask the children if they would like to see it jump into the water.
- Have the children get quiet and count to three.
- Drop the animal into the tub of water with a splash.
- Encourage the children to clap and cheer for each animal as it splashes into the "swimming pool."

(continues)

Animal High-Dive Competition *(continued)*

- Expand on this activity by asking the children to name the kind of dive they want the animal to do, such as "Let the elephant do a double back flip." Do as the children suggest before letting the animal drop into the water.
- End the activity or take it to a higher level by holding a "diving contest" between the animals and have the children be the judges—telling you what type of dive each animal should do and then awarding a score.

Practical Tips

- *If you have time, give each child a paper towel and an animal and have them help dry off the animals. This is a subtle way to get the children involved in clean-up time.*
- *Use your imagination to create similar activities, such as Stuffed Animal Dry-Diving, or Baby Doll Beauty Contest.*

MEMORY

Miniature Car Wash Rampage

OBJECTIVE
To recognize colors and identify parts of a car

APPROXIMATE TIME
5–15 minutes

AGES
3–4

REQUIRED MATERIALS
Several toy cars in a container (cars that change colors when they are wet are great for this activity)
Tub of soapy water
Several toothbrushes—one for each child
Paper towels

- Place the tub of soapy water on a table or counter that the children can reach.
- Hold the container of cars high enough so the children are unable to see into it. One by one, pull a car out of the container and ask the children what color the car is.
- Depending on the children's skill level, ask questions such as: How many wheels do cars have? What are some basic car parts? (windshield, doors, trunk, etc.).

- After the children have responded, put the cars one by one into the tub of soapy water.
- Give each child a toothbrush, and let them all choose a car to wash.
- Have them scrub their cars thoroughly.
- Then give them each a paper towel to dry the cars.
- Finish by having the children place the clean cars back into the container of toy cars.

(continue

Miniature Car Wash Rampage *(continued)*

Practical Tips

- *Use recognition activities like this one to give younger children a better understanding of their surrounding environment.*
- *Mix the questions and the recognition activity with something a little off the wall and energetic. Children enjoy having adults interact with them in this way.*

Body Drawing

Objective
To identify body parts and other things such as clothing

Approximate Time
5–12 minutes

Ages
3–4

Required Materials
Felt-tip markers
Posterboard or butcher paper

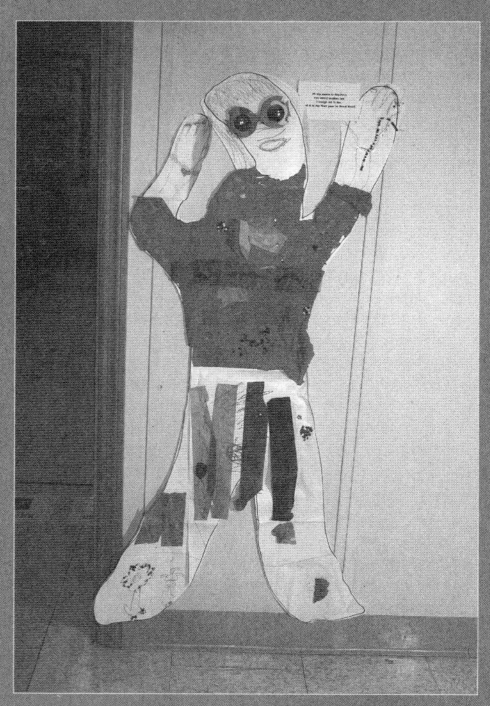

- Tape the posterboard to a visible wall, high enough so the children can't reach it but low enough for them to see it.
- Use a marker to begin drawing a person, from the head down, drawing each detail (eyes, ears, hair, mouth, teeth), and have the children name each part as you draw it.
- Add more items, such as clothes, jewelry, shoes, and so forth.
- Be as creative as you like, and encourage the children to make suggestions as to how and what you draw (size of nose, facial expressions, hair length and style, designs on the person's clothes, and so on).
- As you draw, involve the children further by asking them interactive questions pertaining to what you are drawing. Examples: When you are drawing the shirt, ask those wearing short-sleeved shirts to raise their hand. Have the children point to those who are wearing blue. While drawing the hair, have the children with a certain color or length of hair raise a hand or stand up.
- When you have finished drawing the entire person, draw a background of the children's choosing (based on the time available and the children's attention span)
- Use the poster as a room decoration.

(continues)

Body Drawing *(continued)*

Practical Tips

- *Encourage the children's imagination and creativity by the way you draw.*
- *Involve the children intellectually at their level.*
- *Follow the children's lead, and draw and talk about the things that interest them. Watch their body language to gauge their interest.*

MEMORY

Drawing Things

Objective
To recognize objects and expand vocabulary

Approximate Time	**Ages**
5–15 minutes	3–6

Required Materials
Felt-tip markers
A few pieces of posterboard (or chalk and chalkboard)

- Tape the posterboard to a wall, high enough so the children can't reach it but low enough for them to see it.
- Using a marker, draw objects while encouraging the children to guess what you're drawing. Make the objects and details as simple or as elaborate as you like, depending on the children's age and developmental level.

- Don't limit the drawings to things. Draw people, places—anything else you can think of.
- Have the children shout out their guesses or, if that gets too loud, have them raise their hand and call upon them individually.
- If needed, help the children by giving clues (for example, for a drawing of a cow, moo like a cow, talk about what cows eat, where they live, and so on).
- Occasionally interject new items into the game to keep the children paying attention and enlarge their vocabulary and expand their repertoire of object recognition.

MEMORY

(continues)

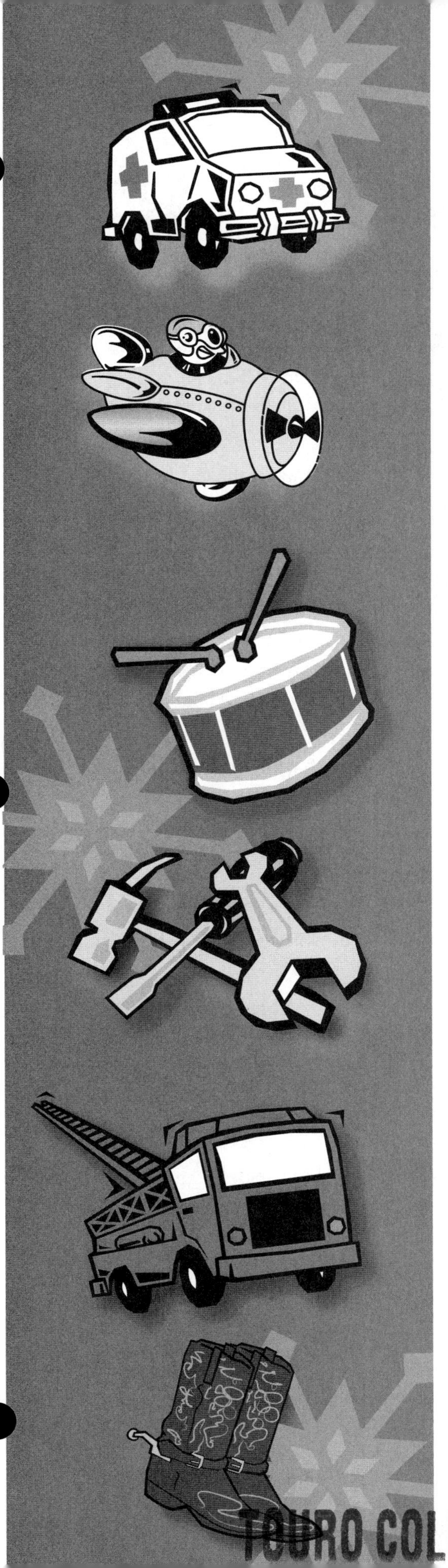

Practical Tips

- *Don't think you have to be an artist. Draw the best you can, and the children will enjoy your efforts.*
- *Search for more and more difficult objects for the children to describe.*

Random Office Supply Highlight

Objective
To recognize objects and develop vocabulary

Approximate Time	Ages
5–7 minutes	3–5

Required Materials
Office supply item (such as a stapler, hole punch, or ruler)

MEMORY

- Select an office item and place it in a cupboard or other hidden place.
- Tell the children it's "Office Supply Time." They won't know what that means, but if you're excited, they will mimic your emotion.
- Pull out the object, tell them its name and function, then demonstrate it for them.
- Depending on the ages of the children and the office supply you choose, allow volunteers to use it—to staple some papers together, use the hole punch, and so on.

Practical Tips

- *Use this activity for other categories, such as "name that tool in the garage" or "name that color of crayon," or "count the number of doors on each car in the parking lot."*

A Visit from Our Friendly Pet . . . Whatever

Objective
To learn the characteristics of specific animals

Approximate Time
7–15 minutes

Ages
3–6

Required Materials
Animal puppet or stuffed animal

- Preferably, use an animal puppet, but a stuffed animal could work.
- Put the animal in a closet or cardboard box ahead of time.
- When it comes time for the activity, tell the children that your pet (whatever you choose to use) is coming to visit.
- Have the children sit quietly while you explain that the animal is shy and will be scared away if the children get too loud or don't stay in their seats.
- Ask the children to count to three with you to "wake up" the pet.
- Do this two or three times, explaining that the animal is a sound sleeper.
- Then pull out the animal and act as if the animal were real, making appropriate animal sounds, petting it, and so on.
- Have the children all greet the animal.

(continues)

MEMORY

A Visit from Our Friendly Pet . . . Whatever *(continued)*

- Ask the children questions about the animal's color, size, and what it does (live in a tree? fly? swim under water? etc.)
- Point to the animal's various body parts—eyes, nose, tail, ears—and have the children identify these parts.
- Bring the pet around and give each child an opportunity to pet it or scratch it behind the ears.
- Hook a leash to a collar on the animal puppet or stuffed animal and allow the children to take turns walking it to lunch or snack

Practical Tips

- *Use this activity in a bus or a van while the children are buckled in their seatbelts. (Set a good example by outwardly buckling your own seatbelt.)*

Objective
To develop recognition and memory skills

Approximate Time
5–7 minutes

Ages
3–5

Required Materials
Stuffed monkey (or any stuffed animal really!)
Wall cabinets, preferably

Cheer for the Monkey

- Place the stuffed animal just inside one of the cabinet doors and seat the children on the floor in front of the cabinet.
- Tell the children that your little hairy friend, Mr. Monkey Munk, was playing hide-and-seek with you earlier and he hid so well that you can't find him.
- Ask the children if they will help you as you look for the monkey by telling you if they see him.
- Slowly look throughout the room.
- Then open the cabinet door with the monkey inside and pretend not to see him. The children will see him and shout and point to let you know.
- Immediately close the cabinet as if their yelling startled you.
- Ask them why they were yelling, and they will tell you they found the monkey. They may try to walk over and point out the location, but they should remain sitting down for this activity.
- Ask them which cabinet the monkey is in
- Point to each cabinet door—except the one the monkey is in.
- Keep playing dumb while they tell you, "No, he's not in there . . . the other one!"
- Finally open the cabinet with the monkey inside. The children probably will laugh and scream.

(continues)

MEMORY

MEMORY

Cheer for the Monkey *(continued)*

- Close the door quickly and ask the children to be quiet, then open the door again and let them yell and laugh.
- Repeat this several times, being sure to act surprised every time you see the monkey.
- At last, open the door and grab the monkey. The children will cheer.
- Allow them to pet the monkey and say "hi."
- When you are finished, have the children say goodbye and put the monkey back in the cabinet.

Practical Tips

- *Use this activity as a good outlet for children's imagination. Their thinking they know something you don't know will enhance their relationship with you.*

Winter or Summer?

Objective
To learn the seasons

Approximate Time
5–10 minutes

Ages
3–5

Required Materials
Large cardboard box
Items or pictures of items representing each season (for example, pictures of a swimming pool, beach, snowman, mittens, hot sun)

- In advance, put all of the winter and summer items into the box.
- Tell the children you want to separate your summer stuff from your winter stuff but you need help. The children will be giddy to help.
- Tell them you're going to take the items out of the box one by one for everyone to see, and they should tell you if the item is used in summer or in winter.
- As they identify each item, divide everything into two piles—summer and winter.
- When you've sorted through everything, select children one at a time to put an item back in the box.

MEMORY

(continues)

Winter or Summer? *(continued)*

Practical Tips

- *Vary this activity for all the seasons. Items and pictures for spring and fall could include seed packets, a leaf rake, leaves. . . . You get the idea.*

Name That Thing

Objective
To recognize objects and colors

Approximate Time
5–12 minutes

Ages
3–6

Required Materials
Large cardboard box
Miscellaneous items—a shoe, some pennies, a doll, a drink container, a stapler, etc.

- In advance, fill the box with an assortment of items and set it out of the children's reach.
- Have all the children sit on the floor.
- When they are all sitting and quiet, tell them you found this big box in your closet filled with all kinds of stuff and you can't wait to show them what's inside it.
- Ask the children what they think is in the box, and encourage them to call out their guesses.
- Answer each guess with "Maybe" or "I don't know?" or "We'll see."
- Ask the children if they would like to see what is in the box (having waited all this time, they will be excited).
- Take the top off the box and slowly pull out an item.
- Ask the children if they know what it is, and ask follow-up questions: What color is it? What is it for? What do you do with it?

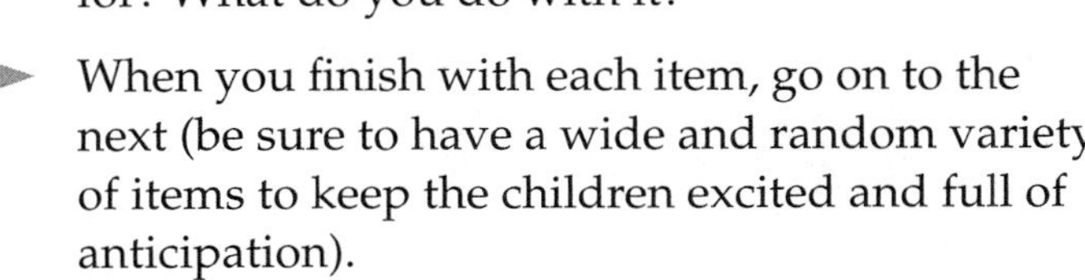

- When you finish with each item, go on to the next (be sure to have a wide and random variety of items to keep the children excited and full of anticipation).

(continues)

Name That Thing *(continued)*

- Go through as many items as time allows. Don't feel pressured into going through all of the items. If you run out of time, save the box for later in the day or a different day.
- For a whole new activity, replace the items in the box.

Practical Tips

- *Give this activity a theme. For example, it could be related to the seasons (see Activity 51)*
- *Tie this activity to another one. For example, if you are going on a fieldtrip soon, include items that relate to that fieldtrip (permission slips, a first-aid kit, keys to the bus, a picture of the place you are going). When you finish, ask the children what these things have in common. You could even use this activity to announce a fieldtrip.*

Name That Shape

Objective
To recognize shapes

Approximate Time
5–12 minutes

Ages
3–6

Required Materials
Several sheets of construction paper of four or five different colors
Scissors

- Treat this activity like a game show. (Optional: Dress up in a blazer, tie, wig, and funny glasses.) Say, "Who wants to play 'Name That Shape?'"
- Get the children all pumped up, then tell them how the game works.
- Start cutting out a shape (which you have drawn in advance) from a sheet of construction paper. Let the children see you cutting but not the shape itself.

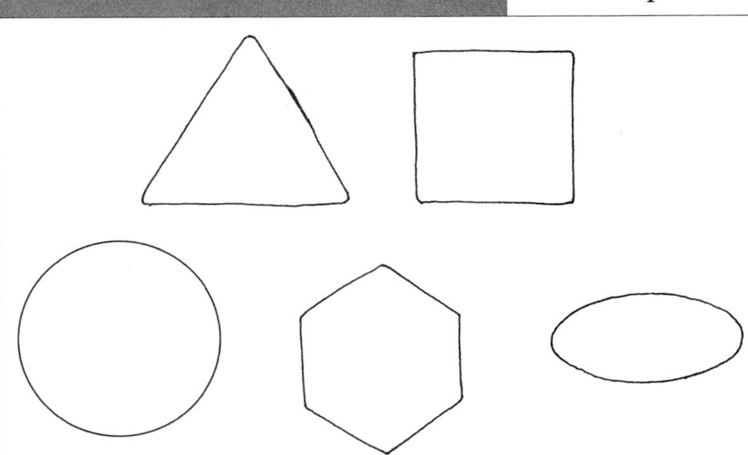

- Hum while you are cutting to make time pass, but try to cut quickly
- Once the shape is cut out, hold it up and ask, "Who knows what shape this is?"
- Obtain their answers in a couple of different ways:
  - Have all the children answer in unison—which helps the activity run more quickly. If all the children don't know the shapes, some children will dominate the activity.
  - Select a different child each time to try first to identify each shape. This will give everyone a chance to answer, and you can give hints if needed.

(continues)

MEMORY

MEMORY

Name That Shape *(continued)*

- To expand this activity, take all the cut-out shapes and ask the children to compare them. Ask the children what color each of them is, and so forth.
- As a variation, cut the shapes to different sizes and ask which shapes are bigger or smaller.

Practical Tips

- *Use this versatile activity with younger children who are first learning about shapes, as well as colors, sizes, comparisons, and similar concepts. This activity is a good one to demonstrate to children that they can have fun while they learn.*
- *Use your creativity in dressing up like the game show host. This brings the game to life.*

Missing Person

Objective
To enhance memory

Approximate Time
5–7 minutes

Ages
3–6

Required Materials
Blanket, or a box big enough for several children to hide under it

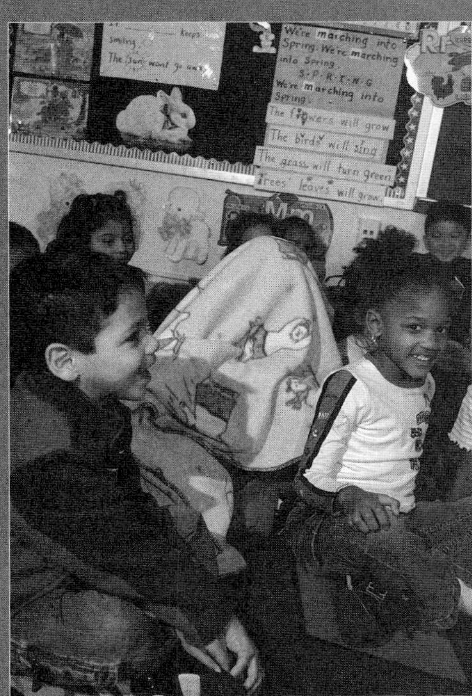

- With everyone sitting in a circle, tell the children they are going to play a game called "Missing Person."
- Tell the children that to begin this game, they have to know everyone's name in the group.
- Point to one child and say his or her name.
- Have all the children say the name with you.
- After going around the circle several times (don't forget yourself!), randomly around the circle say the names of different children. Tell the children that this is where the game gets harder.
- Have the children close their eyes while you put the blanket or box over someone in the circle.
- Have the children open their eyes. Ask who is missing and let them guess until they get it right. If they name someone who is still in the circle, say something like, "No it can't be Desiree because she's right there. Who is missing?"
- Make sure everyone gets a turn to be the missing person.
- Now hide more than one child at a time, but don't tell the others at first that more than one person is gone.
- Finally, hide the whole class or group at once.

(continues)

Missing Person *(continued)*

Practical Tips

- *Because children are often frightened by the unknown, have a teacher or other adult be the first one to be "missing" so the children understand the activity.*

MEMORY

Objective
To recognize colors and patterns

Approximate Time
5–15 minutes

Ages
3–6

Required Materials
The students' clothes they are wearing
Or a box of dress-up clothes

55 Just What Do You Think You're Wearing, Young Lady?!

- Pick a child and have him or her stand in front of the class (most children want to do this, so you might want to lengthen the time, or you could repeat the activity as often as needed to include everyone.
- Ask the other children about what the child is wearing and descriptive questions about the clothing: "Is Suzie wearing shorts or pants? Are pants longer or shorter than shorts? What color is Andy's shirt?" If an item of the child's clothing has a pattern, ask about it and the colors in it.
- Ask the children other specific questions: "Does Suzie have long or short hair? What color are her eyes? What is Andy wearing on his feet?" Be as detailed as you can. This is a good way to teach items of clothing (buttons, zippers, collars, etc.).
- End the activity by commenting that each child is unique right down to the clothes he or she wears.

(continues)

Just What Do You Think You're Wearing, Young Lady?! *(continued)*

Practical Tips

- *Be as simple or as detailed as the age of the group warrants. With younger children, you'll want to move from child to child more quickly.*
- *As another variation, have a box of dress-up clothes and begin layering a child with the clothing items, describing each one as it is added.*

Scrub-a-Dub Time

Objective
To learn the importance of keeping things clean

Approximate Time
5–12 minutes

Ages
3–6

Required Materials
Paper towels
A water spray bottle (more if you can get them)

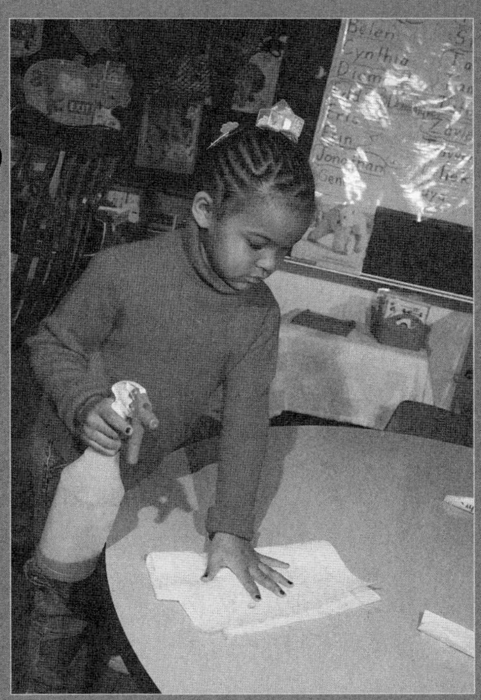

- Tell the children you want to clean up the classroom and you need their help to do it.
- Give each child a paper towel.
- If you have enough spray bottles, have two or three children share each bottle.
- Have the children go around the room and clean different things. Have them spray the wall, floors, windows, etc. and wipe them down.
- Have them clean the little "nooks and crannies" of the room—door knobs, mirrors, and the like.
- Let the children replace their paper towel as they need to, and encourage them to pretend they are grown-ups.
- As the activity winds down and the children are looking for more things to clean, suggest different areas (the children will rush to whatever you mention).

Practical Tips

- *Before or after the activity, tell the children they can look for ways to help mom or dad around the house, such as by keeping their toys picked up.*

From a young age, teach children the importance of keeping things clean and how to participate. We frequently wait until children are much older, but this need not be. A three-year-old can learn to pick up toys or clean off a tabletop.

Repetition

The activities in this category:

- Use repetitive listing of certain information.
- Are memory-enhancing activities that will help the children concentrate and work the memory center of their brain.
- Are especially good with younger children but can be useful with some older children, too.

Elvis and the Animals

OBJECTIVE
To exercise memory skills

APPROXIMATE TIME	AGES
5–10 minutes	3–8

REQUIRED MATERIALS
Several stuffed animals (the more exotic the better)
A doll or small plastic figure of some kind (representing the hero of the story you will tell)
Paper and pencils for the children to make lists

- Gather the animals (four or five for younger children and six to 10 for older children). The size of the animals doesn't matter.
- Introduce the hero of the story (the doll or plastic figure), who should have a silly name (such as "fuzzy-haired Billy Bockentickerhead").
- Tell the children that our hero has many pets, and bring out the stuffed animals—polar bear, zebra, pelican, giraffe—whatever you have.

- If the children are old enough, have them fill in three lists as you tell the story: the animals, the places Billy looks for the animals, and the things he does when he gets home each night. Allow time for the children to write down this information.
- Repeat the information in the same order every time. As you continue to repeat the story lines and add information, the children will be telling more of the story and you will be telling less.
- Start the story:
  - Every day when he gets up, our hero has to go out and feed his animals. He feeds [his polar bear, his zebra, his pelican, his giraffe] always in the same order.

(continues)

REPETITION

Elvis and the Animals *(continued)*

- By the time he finishes feeding them, the day is over, so he goes in the house, has dinner, reads a book, brushes his teeth, and goes to bed (put as many things on this list as you want).
- The next morning he gets up to feed his pet animals (hide the last animal on the list beforehand), and says, "Hey, one of the animals is missing. Who is missing?"
- Fuzzy-haired Billy Bockentickerhead is really upset and goes looking for his missing (the kids will shout "giraffe!" or whatever animal you have hidden) in the imaginary desert, the mountains, the forest, the jungle, the ocean, the river—but he can't find his missing (the kids will call out its name again) anywhere.
- By now it is getting late and Billy is tired and hungry, so he goes home to have dinner, read a book, brush his teeth, and go to bed. (Repeat the entire list of things he does befo bedtime, in the same order.)

► Continue telling the story. With each passing day, one more animal is missing.

- Finally, Billy comes out one morning and sees that no animals are left, so he searches for them in all of the places he searched before.
- On the day when Billy finds all the animals missing, he sees a long-haired, overweight man with long sideburns wearing a white, sequined jumpsuit leaving the barn where the animals were kept.
- Fuzzy-haired Billy Bockentickerhead chases the man (you guessed it) through the desert, the mountains, the forest, the jungle, the ocean, the river, and finally to a big cave.
- The cave is full of neon lights and pinball machines, and all the animals are there eating french fries.

(contin

Elvis and the Animals *(continued)*

- Fuzzy-haired Billy Bockentickerhead finds out that Elvis has been hiding in this cave since 1977, and he was lonely, so he invited Billy's animals to visit him in his cave.
- Now fuzzy-haired Billy Bockentickerhead invites Elvis to eat dinner with him. They and all the animals (have the children say them all in order) go back to Billy's house and have dinner, read a book, brush their teeth, and all go to bed.

Practical Tips

- *Build on the knowledge that children like repetitious stories.*
- *Encourage the children to add to the story if they like.*
- *Vary the story by changing the animals or the places Billy looks for them (try the glacier, the rain forest, the tundra, the Hawaiian Islands—or whatever faraway place you can think of).*

58

Name That Class

Objective
To strengthen memory skills

Approximate Time
5–10 minutes

Ages
3–8

Required Materials
NONE

- Introduce the activity: "We're going to play 'Name that Class!'"
- Go around the room and have each child say his or her name.
- Now have the class say the names together as you point to each child.
- Say the names faster and faster.
- Have the children close their eyes and repeat the names in the same order.

Practical Tips

- *As a variation on this game, move one child to the end of the group. The children are to leave his or her name in the same place on the list of children but also add him on the end as well. Do this randomly until every child's name is used twice (or three times).*

REPETITION

Last Night for Dinner I Had . . .

Objective
To expand memory and creativity

Approximate Time
5–10 minutes

Ages
3–10

Required Materials
NONE

- In this "finish the sentence" activity, have the first person say, "Last night for dinner I had . . . turkey" (or whatever).

- Have the second person repeat what the first one said and add something like: "Last night for dinner I had . . . turkey and pizza."
- Have the third person repeat the first two things and add one more. . . . and so on.
- Continue until each child has had a turn or the list is so ridiculous or so long that you have to start over.

Practical Tips

- *Encourage the children to be silly and come up with strange food combinations.*
- *Laugh with the children about the weird dinners they come up with.*

REPETITION

Today When I Woke Up, I . . .

Objective
To strengthen memory and creativity

Approximate Time	**Ages**
5–10 minutes	3–10

Required Materials
NONE

- Have the children state what they did when they got up in the morning. Items could include, for example: I combed my hair, walked the dog, ate breakfast, and so on.

Practical Tips

- *Vary this activity—which is basically the same as Activity 59—in limitless ways. Try "When school is out, I want to . . ." or "On vacation I . . ." or "Every night before bed I . . . ." You get the idea.*
- *Have the children think up the scenarios, too. They will enjoy it even more knowing that the concept was their idea.*

Character Sketch/ Role-Play

The activities in this category are intended to:

- Encourage the children to become involved in role-play as participants or observers.
- Possibly include one of the teachers, or a visitor, dressing up as a character and acting out one or more of the roles.
- Give the children information about specific jobs and functions in life.
- Be educational or simply fun.
- Involve a lot of imagination and pretending but are different from the Imagination category in their emphasis on jobs and roles.
- Suggest props for the most part but can be done anywhere without props.
- Have the teacher take the age group into account in the descriptions and details.

Note: Because this category involves role-play, the character involved is included in parentheses, when helpful.

63

Objective
To learn how X-ray procedures are done

Approximate Time	**Ages**
10–20 minutes	3–8

Materials
White doctor's coat (and wig if you want to look really different)
Old X ray of anyone or anything
Clipboard
Overhead projector or bright spotlight
Heavy old coat

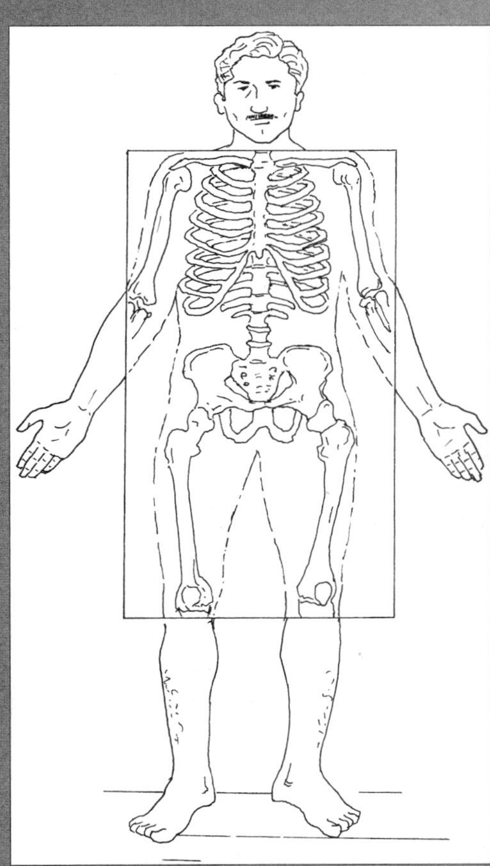

Mr. X-ray Picture Guy (a tribute to radiologists everywhere)

- Dress up in the doctor's coat and pretend to be a special guest radiologist.
- Ask the children if any of them has ever had an X ray taken before.
- Tell them that an X ray is a picture of the inside of our body, and it is the way a doctor can look at our bones and organs that we can't see through our skin.
- Ask for a volunteer to assist in your demonstration, and have the rest of the children pretend they are getting an X ray, too.
- Have the volunteer come in front of the class, and position him or her in different funny ways:
  - Have the child lift one leg and hold it in the air, then say "No, that's not right."
  - Have the child lift one arm in the air and touch the knee with the other hand, and say, "No, that's not right either."
  - Do this four or five times, putting the child in a different funny position each time (followed by your saying in a puzzled tone, "No, that's still not right").
- Finally have the child stand up straight, hands by the sides, facing the class, and say "There we go—that's it."

(continues)

ROLE-PLAY

Mr. X-ray Picture Guy (a tribute to radiologists everywhere) *(continued)*

- Tell the child to stand absolutely still because you are going to take a picture.
- Put on the heavy old coat backward (so the zipper or buttons are in the back), then run and hide at the back of the room.
- While you are there, have another teacher or helper turn on the spotlight or overhead projector and then turn it off again immediately. (If you can't get a spotlight or an overhead projector, go to the back of the room and turn the lights off and back on.)
- Conclude this activity by talking about the reason the radiologist leaves the room when taking the X ray. Assure the children that it is safe because they are having an X ray only one once in a while, but radiologists take many X rays every day, so they have to protect themselves so they don't get sick.
- Tell the children that when they will get an X ray of their mouth someday, the dental hygienist will put the heavy "blanket" on them. This information might help them relax so they don't get scared when it happens to them.
- Pull out the old X ray and say, "I think we've found the problem. It looks like you must have swallowed an elephant!"

Practical Tips

- *Ask a local doctor or radiologist if he or she would be willing to donate an old X ray for this activity.*
- *Ask a local radiologist to do the character sketch for you. If you bring in someone from the outside, the activity will change from a transition activity to a planned learning activity—fine!*

Is My Medicine Ready Yet? (pharmacist)

Objective
To learn what prescription medications are and how they are used

Approximate Time
10–20 minutes

Ages
3–6

Materials
White coat or jacket
Pill-counting board
Beads (to teach the children about counting but *not* something that could be confused for pills)
Empty medicine bottles
An old phone

- Put on a white coat and pretend to be a special guest pharmacist.
- Ask the children if any of them have gone to the pharmacy with someone to get medicine.
- Tell them that medicine is helpful when we are sick but we should take it only when our doctor or mom or dad tells us to. Depending on the ages and children's readiness, you could talk about the difference between drugs and medication: Drugs are something bad you might try to take on your own, or medicine that has not been prescribed for you. Medication is something a doctor tells us to take or our mom or dad gets from the pharmacy for us.

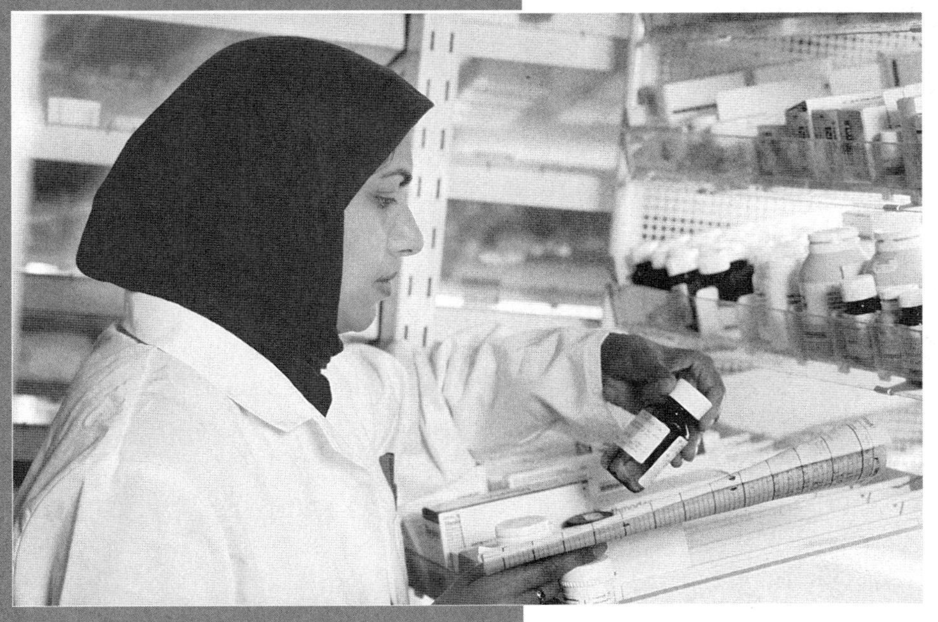

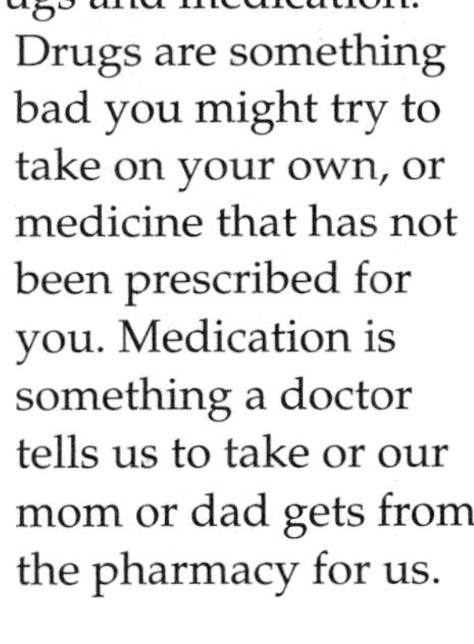

ROLE-PLAY

(continues)

Is My Medicine Ready Yet? (pharmacist) *(continued)*

- Talk about how important it is for our mom or dad to read the labels and always follow the instructions.
- Tell the children that pharmacists go to school for a long time to study medications and how they can help us get better if we're sick. Tell them they should never take any medicine without being told because this would be like taking poison.
- Answer the imaginary ring of the phone.
- Have a short conversation with an imaginary doctor who is calling in someone's prescription, or talk to someone who is checking to see if the medicine is ready. (You could say, "Okay, Dr. Jones. That's two of the green get-better pills a day for Mr. Yoohoo. I'll make sure he understands not to take them while he's driving his car," or "Yes, Mrs. Bla-Bla. Your doctor called earlier and your prescription is ready. I'll have the delivery boy bring it over."
- Use the pill counting board to count out some of the beads into the medicine bottles.
- Conclude this activity by telling the children that if they find a medication bottle, they should give it to their mom or dad immediately, and they should tell an adult right away if they (or a friend) swallow pills that didn't come from a doctor or their parents.
- Have a volunteer help you fill bottles with the beads (if the children are old enough so they wouldn't put them in their mouth and they have the necessary fine motor skills to handle these small objects).

(continue

Is My Medicine Ready Yet? (pharmacist) *(continued)*

Practical Tips

- *Ask a local pharmacist if he or she is willing to donate empty medicine bottles or other props that would help with the role-play, or ask a friend who works in a pharmacy and could help out.*
- *Ask a pharmacist if you can borrow a pill-sorter, as this is a unique device that most children would not have seen.*
- *Invite a local pharmacist to do the character sketch as a guest. (This will change the activity from a transition to a planned learning activity.)*

I Think There's Something Wrong with My Car (auto mechanic)

Objective
To learn something about cars, tools that auto mechanics use, and what mechanics do

Approximate Time
10–20 minutes

Ages
3–6

Materials
A pair of coveralls to fit you
A smaller pair of coveralls for the volunteer, or an apron
A large play car
Tools—wrench, tire gauge, can of motor oil; old engine parts

ROLE-PLAY

- Dress up in the coveralls and pretend to be a special guest mechanic.
- Ask the children if any of them have had to take their car to the shop to have it fixed (of course, they will say they have!).
- Ask what they had fixed, and respond that your (same part) broke, too.
- Tell them you are a mechanic and you have come to work on the car in front of them.
- Ask for a volunteer to be your assistant mechanic.
- Get another volunteer to be the car owner.
- Dress up the volunteer mechanic in an outfit like yours, including an apron if you have it, and let the child hold one of the tools.
- With the "car owner" sitting in the car, have him or her explain to you how the car has been acting.
- Respond by saying something like, "That must be your muffler bearing" or "I think we should grease up those brakes really good, and that should fix the problem." Be sure to ask your "assistant" for advice.
- Have the "car owner" "start" the car and make the engine noise.

(continu

I Think There's Something Wrong with My Car (auto mechanic) *(continued)*

- Say something like, "Quick—shut it off! Shut it off! That sounds really bad."
- Have your "assistant" get down on the floor as close as possible to being under it.
- Have the assistant get up, and you get down there.
- Let your "assistant" hand you real or pretend tools, and act like you are doing something. Say things like, "Let me see if I can tighten this . . . oh, no . . . yeah, there it is."
- End this activity by telling the children that you really like your job as a mechanic because you like taking stuff apart and putting it back together again.
- Discuss with the children how some dads or moms are very good at fixing cars and other dads or moms aren't good with mechanical things—which is okay because we aren't all alike.
- Make your exit by saying that you need to get back to the shop to work on the transmission of the Farckles' Buick.

Practical Tips

- *As an alternative, invite an auto mechanic to come to the class to talk about and demonstrate the tools.*
- *If you can't get your hands on a large toy car, use a tricycle or a bicycle.*
- *If you really want to get into the role, rub some face paint on your face and hands to make it look like you have been working on cars all day.*

My Toilet Won't Flush (plumber)

Objective
To learn what a plumber does

Approximate Time
10–20 minutes

Ages
3–6

Materials
A pair of coveralls for yourself
A toilet plunger
Heavy-duty (or rubber) gloves
Apron
Face mask
Marking pens or waterpaints

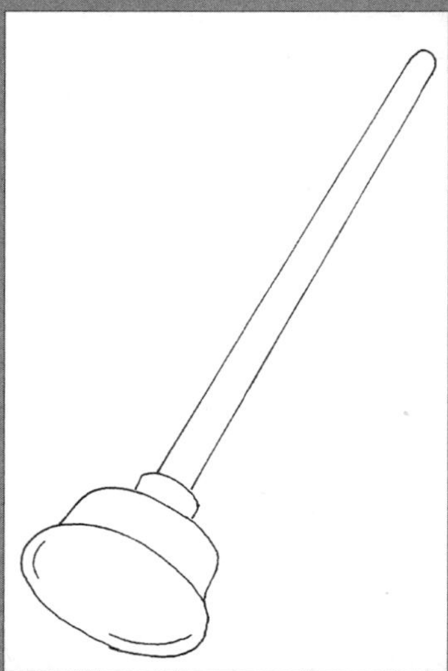

- Dress up in coveralls and announce that you are a special guest plumber.
- Put on the rubber gloves and have the face mask hanging around your neck. Don't actually wear the face mask, because the children wouldn't be able to hear or understand you.
- Ask the children if any of them have ever had a plumber come to their house before.
- After the chorus of "me!" explain what a plumber does and that some plumbers work on new houses and businesses and others go into existing homes and businesses to fix leaky faucets and clogged toilets.
- Ask for a volunteer to become your plumber's helper, and have him or her put on the huge rubber gloves, an apron, and a face mask.
- Tell the children you were called to their class to fix a clogged toilet.
- Have all the children put on their imaginary apron, rubber gloves, and face mask.
- Have your plumber's helper take the plunger and help you plunge. Say things like, "Wow, this is a tough clog" or "Man, you don't want to be downwind of that very long."
- Make toilet-plunging sounds from your imaginary toilet (swish, blub blub blub, gurgle gurgle gurgle, swish).

(continue

My Toilet Won't Flush (plumber) *(continued)*

- Ask the children to stand up and work with you on the imaginary toilet with their imaginary toilet plungers, and have them make the swishing sounds along with you.
- When the imaginary clog begins to loosen, lead the children in cheering and clapping (excited at your victory over the clog!).
- End this activity by telling the children you like your job as a plumber and feel important because you keep busy fixing broken sinks and clogged toilets and installing new ones. Besides, your customers are very happy to have the problem fixed.
- Exit after an emergency phone call that you answer, saying: "Well, I'm off to save another . . ."

Practical Tips

- *Use markers or paint to make greasy-looking marks on the coveralls.*
- *Although props are suggested for this activity because they are usually available, don't skip the activity if you can't get them. It just takes even more imagination.*
- *Emphasize to the children that they should not do this at home without talking to their mom or dad first.*

My House Needs To Be Fixed (carpenter)

Objective
To learn what a carpenter does and what remodeling is

Approximate Time
10–20 minutes

Ages
3–6

Materials
Tool belt (the bigger the better—the belt should either be so full of tools you can hardly lift it or it should be oversized with only one screwdriver in it)
Big rubber gloves
Old blueprints (if you can locate them)
Toy phone

ROLE-PLAY

- Put on the tool belt and pretend to be a special guest carpenter.
- Ask the children if any of them know someone who builds or fixes houses (many hands will go up).
- Explain what a home builder and a carpenter do: Some carpenters work on new houses and businesses, and others go into existing homes and businesses and fix or remodel things.
- Depending on the age group, introduce the concept of *remodeling* and have the children repeat the word until they get it right.
- Ask for a volunteer to be your helper, and have him or her put on the huge leather gloves and tool belt, or ask the volunteer to hold the biggest tool you can find (one that no child in the class could lift) for you for a few minutes while you talk to the other children (make sure the tool isn't dangerous to the children). Really talk it up to the children while you pretend not to pay attention to the struggling helper.
- Tell the children you were called to their class to fix something that is broken or to plan a remodeling job.
- If you have blueprints, go around the room and look at various things, then look back at the blueprints. Say something like, "Yes, I see. . . .

(continued)

My House Needs To Be Fixed (carpenter) *(continued)*

Okay, we could move this wall and knock a hole in that one and then move this over there and put down some wood flooring and . . . "

- Have the children put on their imaginary tool belts and pretend to help.
- Involve your helper and the entire class by asking for their advice. Encourage them to use their imagination.
- Walk around with one of the tools and lightly hit on things, saying "Aha! Oh my . . . well, we'll see about that."
- End this activity by telling the children that you really like your job because you get to use your imagination and try to picture things differently than they are.
- Tell them you enjoy helping people and seeing how good things look after you finish your work.
- Tell them there is always a need for people to fix broken things and help remodel old houses.
- At the conclusion, answer an imaginary phone call and say, "Well I'm off to have a look at my next job."

Practical Tips

- *As with the other activities in this category, do this one with or without props. In either case, the children's imagination will come to the fore.*
- *If you don't have blueprints, make some pretend ones by rolling up white bulletin board paper.*

Could You Use a Loan? (banker)

Objective
To learn something about a banker's job

Approximate Time
10–20 minutes

Ages
3–6

Materials
A clipboard
An old checkbook or wallet
Play money

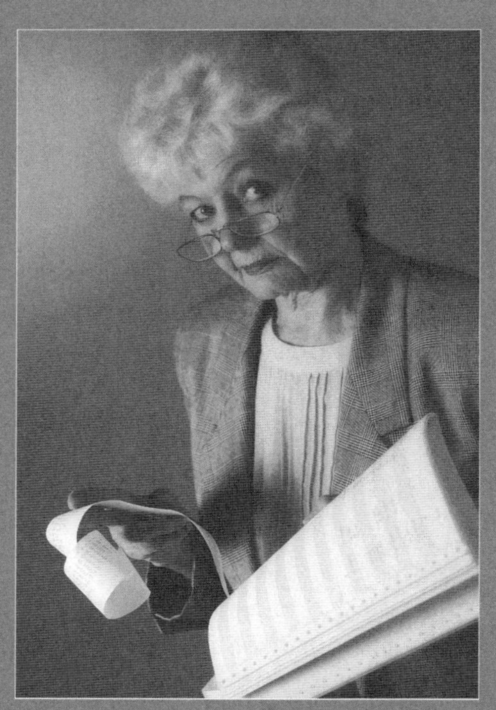

- Pretend to be a special guest banker and ask the children if any of them know someone who works in a bank for a living (expect a large response).
- Explain that some people who work in a bank are called tellers and that they make change, help people deposit money in their accounts, and cash checks.
- Go on to another role in a bank—the loan officer, who lends people money to buy homes, cars, and other large purchases. He or she will explain that the money isn't yours forever. You have to pay it back.
- Ask the children to pretend that their class is a large family and say that you are there today to help them get a loan for a new house.
- Ask the children questions like how much income they earn, where they work, how many children they have, and questions about their house—how many bedrooms and bathrooms they need, and so on.
- Take notes and fill out a "loan application" on your clipboard.
- End this activity by telling the children you have to go back to the bank and get on the computer to fill out some forms, do a credit check, and present the loan to a committee to make the final decision.

(continue

Could You Use a Loan? (banker) *(continued)*

- Take this opportunity to talk about the word "committee." Explain that this is a group of people who meet to make decisions or give advice about things; that many organizations have committees, such as the bank and their child care center.

Practical Tips

- *Fit this activity to the age group with which you are working. The concepts of money, cost, committees, loans, and the like, although complex, are appropriate for children of all ages. They have the capacity to understand that things cost money, that people work for money, and so on.*

Objective
To learn about work in a fast-food place

Approximate Time
10–20 minutes

Ages
3–6

Materials
Paper cups
Empty french fry or hamburger containers
Something that could serve as a cash register

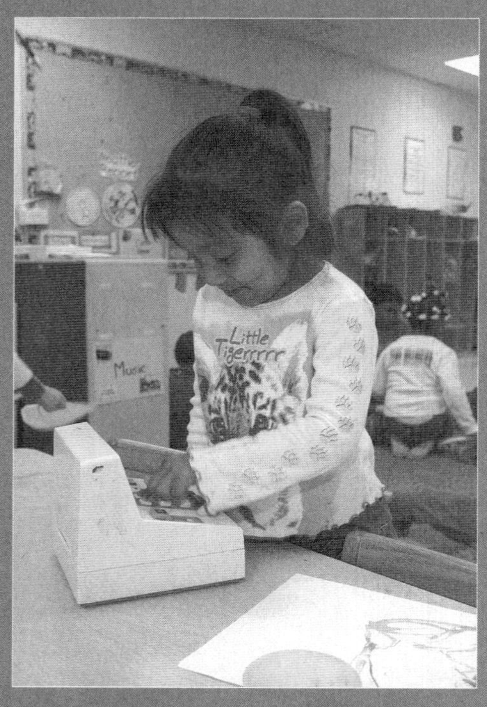

ROLE-PLAY

Are You Going To Eat Those Fries? (fast-food server)

- Begin by asking the children if they have ever been to a fast-food restaurant (expect a unanimous response).
- Ask them what fast-food restaurant workers do, and help them think up answers such as the person who takes their order inside, the drive-through person, the boss, the person who cooks the fries and hamburgers.
- Inform the children that "we are going to pretend we are at a fast-food restaurant and we need to make sure all of the jobs get done." Each of them should decide which of the jobs mentioned above they want to do.
- Ask the children to act out for you what each of those workers would do. Encourage discussion as the class acts out the various roles.
- As the entire class plays fast-food restaurant, allow them to change jobs if they like.
- Pretend to be a customer and let them wait on you.
- End this activity by telling the children that it is closing time and we have to do the special jobs to close down for the night. Have them suggest and carry out the activities they think would have to be done before leaving.

(continues)

Are You Going To Eat Those Fries? (fast-food server) *(continued)*

Practical Tips

- *Assemble a container of fast-food restaurant stuff—cups, containers, drinking straws, paper hats, etc. Usually fast-food restaurants are open to donating items such as these if you explain why you want them.*
- *Once you've created a "fast-food restaurant kit," use it as a transition activity in the future, or as a learning/play center.*

Why Don't You Try a Size 72? (shoe salesperson)

Objective
To better understand a shoe salesperson's job

Approximate Time	**Ages**
10–20 minutes	3–6

Materials
Several shoe boxes of different sizes
Shoes of various types and sizes
Shoe horn
Child-size chair
Step stool
Play money

- Tell the children they have been magically transported to a local shoe store and you are the shoe salesperson.
- Discuss how important it is to get shoes that fit right and that having shoes that don't fit correctly can cause problems in other places in your body, such as your back.

- Emphasize the importance of the shoe salespersons' job because these workers are specially trained to fit shoes that will contribute to the person's total well-being.
- Ask for a volunteer to come and be your customer, and have the child sit in the chair.
- Sit on the step stool, look at the child's feet, then have him or her stand up and pretend a foot is in one of those foot "sizers" so you can figure out exactly how big the foot is. (You might say something like, "That's the biggest foot I've ever seen!")
- Bring out boxes and boxes of shoes for the "customer" to try on, and have the child walk

(continues)

ROLE-PLAY

Why Don't You Try a Size 72? (shoe salesperson) *(continued)*

around. Say things like, "That shoe is really YOU!"

- Have the child choose a pair of shoes and pretend to pay for them.
- If you have time, give every child a chance to be the customer. If you run out of time, take down names of those who didn't get a turn and tell them they will be first the next time you do this activity.
- Depending on age and interest, ask for volunteers to be the salesperson.
- End this activity by telling the children it is closing time for the store and ask them to help you pick up the shoes and put them in the boxes.

Practical Tips

- *Use this activity (depending on age level) as an opportunity for the children to practice tying shoes.*
- *Have the children practice helping each other take off their shoes and then put them back on. This will teach cooperation as well as hand–eye coordination.*
- *Build a dramatic play center for this activity that you can use again and again.*

Thanks for Calling Smith, Smith, Johnston, and Smith (receptionist)

OBJECTIVE
To better understand a receptionist's job

APPROXIMATE TIME
10–20 minutes

AGES
3–8

MATERIALS
If available, a toy phone for each child—all or none
"While you were out" pads
Pencils or crayons (depending upon age)

- Tell the children you are from a big office building downtown and you are looking for a receptionist.
- Ask the children if they know what a receptionist does, and get their responses.

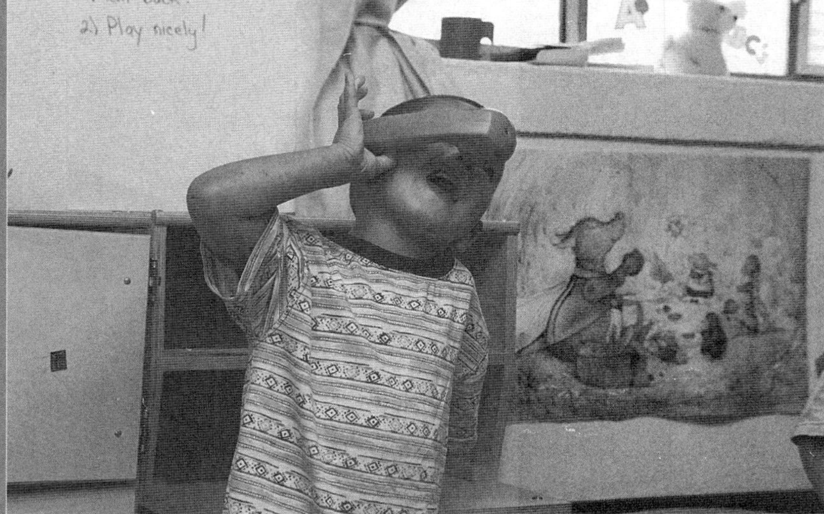

- Explain that a receptionist is someone who works at a company answering the phone and forwarding calls, announcing that people have arrived for their appointments, and similar tasks.
- Depending on how many phones or props you have, ask for one or more volunteers to apply for the job and have them show you how they would do the job. Guide them as they pretend to answer and forward phone calls and take messages.
- End this activity by telling the children that one of the nice things about the receptionist job is that receptionists get to meet and talk to a lot of people both on the phone and in person, and

(continued)

ROLE-PLAY

Thanks for Calling Smith, Smith, Johnston, and Smith (receptionist) *(continued)*

they get to help everyone in the building get their phone calls.

- Discuss the idea of acting like a receptionist when someone calls their home and asks for someone who isn't there. Talk about phone etiquette.

Practical Tips

- *Emphasize that every job is important, whether you are the company president or the receptionist.*
- *Encourage a work ethic and the importance of finding a career or job that makes them feel good about their work.*

Hey, Your Yard Is on Fire! (firefighter)

Objective
To learn about a firefighter's job

Approximate Time
10–20 minutes

Ages
3–8

Materials
Firefighter's hat and coat
Miniature fire truck or rescue vehicle

- Put on the hat and coat and ask the children if any of them know someone who is a firefighter.
- Ask them what a firefighter does, and make sure they understand the basic role of firefighters.
- If any of the children has seen a fire truck respond to a grass fire or a building fire, ask the child to tell about it.
- Take some time to talk about how firefighters are called out for things besides fires—auto accidents, emergency/ambulance calls, and so on. Mention that firefighters are considered some of the real heroes of our society because it's a risky job.
- Invite the children to ask questions about firefighters, and have them tell you what they know about firefighters' work. They may get side-tracked and talk about firefighters in movies they've seen, or books they've read, or firefighters' uniforms, or fire poles—but that's okay.
- Tell the children you like your job a lot because you get to help people when they are

(continues)

Hey, Your Yard Is on Fire! (firefighter) *(continued)*

in trouble. You know your job is dangerous, but it is worth it to you because you help people be safe. Even though people may say firefighters are heroes, you're just doing your job.

- Bring things to a close by receiving an imaginary call and announcing, "Well, I'm off to another emergency."

Practical Tips

- *Take this opportunity to discuss fire alarms and fire drills so the children aren't frightened by the sound of the fire alarm and understand why drills are important.*
- *If you can, get a firefighter to visit the class in full gear (including oxygen mask). This goes beyond a transition, but real-live firefighters would be especially helpful for this activity.*
- *Consider a fieldtrip to a fire station. Most will welcome a visit from your class. This activity is a good one to do before or after such a visit.*

How Fast Were You Going? (police officer)

Objective
To learn about the role of police officers

Approximate Time
10–20 minutes

Ages
3–8

Materials
Police officer's hat and badge
Fake handcuffs
Miniature police car

- Put on the hat and badge, and ask the children if they know a man or woman who is a police officer.
- Discuss the role of police officers to protect us and keep us safe.
- Ask the children about different things a police officer does—directing traffic, issuing tickets, arresting people who do bad things, and helping out during accidents and emergencies.
- Point out that they should yell for a police officer if they get separated from their parents and lost or someone is trying to hurt them.
- Discuss the related job of security guards in malls and other places, whose role is similar in some ways to that of police officers, and advise the children to ask these uniformed people for help if they need it.
- Tell the children that you like your job because you get to protect people from bad things. Say that you know your job is dangerous and some people think policemen are heroes but you're just doing your job.
- Conclude the activity by getting an imaginary call or saying, "Well, I have to get back and keep our streets safe."

(continu

How Fast Were You Going? (police officer) *(continued)*

Practical Tips

- *Invite a police officer to visit the class in uniform, as it is helpful for children to see what police officers look like close up.*
- *Plan a fieldtrip to a police station. Most stations welcome these visits, and this is a good activity to do either before or after that trip.*
- *While you are talking about police officers, some negative comments might come up. Take control and stress that police are doing their jobs and they are here for our protection.*

Atten-HUT! (soldier)

Objective
To learn about some military roles

Approximate Time
10–20 minutes

Ages
3–8

Materials
Camouflage uniform
Toy Humvee, if available

- Put on the uniform and ask the children if they've ever seen people dressed in camouflage uniforms.
- Inform the children that you were sent from the army to see if any of them want to join the army and serve their country. The children probably will respond by wanting to talk about people they know who are serving in the armed services. This is a good opportunity to let them talk.
- Talk to the children about the different branches of the military—National Guard, Reserves, Coast Guard, etc.—and their different roles, such as fighting to protect our country, being stationed on ships, or helping in disasters such as floods or tornadoes.
- Discuss what is required to be accepted into and remain in the military, such as basic training and regular drills.
- Do simple exercises, and have the children line up and march (this also could serve as a large motor skills activity to burn up some energy).
- Invite the children to ask questions about war or times of national security. They may need help understanding and dealing with things they have seen on television or heard adults talking about.

(continue

Atten-HUT! (soldier) *(continued)*

- End the activity by telling the children you like your job because you get to help people by protecting them and providing security to our country. Tell them you know your job is dangerous but it is worth it because you help people feel safe.
- Say, "Well, I'm back to the base to train some new recruits."

Practical Tips

- *Invite a member of the National Guard or Army Reserve or other military branch to visit your class in full uniform. This would go beyond a transition activity, but it is helpful for children to see and hear soldiers close up.*
- *Plan a fieldtrip to a military facility. Most National Guard bases allow tours and might even let the children climb on some large equipment such as a Humvee or a tank. This is an excellent activity to do before or after such a visit. The military hasn't always been popular, but this is an opportunity to create a spirit of patriotism and thank those in the military for the service they give to us and our country.*

ROLE-PLAY

75

Could I Get You a Pillow or Some Peanuts? (flight attendant)

Objective
To better understand the role of a flight attendant and become more comfortable with flying

Approximate Time
10–20 minutes

Ages
3–8

Materials
Pictures of airplanes
Pretzels and juice
A small paper drinking cup
An 18-inch piece of string
8 × 11 card stock
An apron

- Do this activity during snack time.
- To prepare for this activity:
  - Hang pictures of airplanes around the room.
  - Punch two holes near the top of the paper cup equal distance from each other; run the string through the holes, and tie (you will use this later to demonstrate the oxygen mask).
  - Draw some pictures of planes and exit doors on the card stock, and fold it in half vertically (this will be the airplane emergency information card).

- Ask the children how many of them have ever flown in an airplane, then tell them you are going to take an imaginary trip on an airplane during snack time today.
- Announce that they have just boarded an airplane on the way to a fun park (or a tropical island, or wherever). Ask everybody to "please take your seat." (You could have them sit in rows on the floor or in their chairs.)

(continued)

Could I Get You a Pillow or Some Peanuts? (flight attendant) *(continued)*

- Inform the children that you are the flight attendant and you are there to help them have a comfortable flight. Before you get started, you will give them safety instructions: "Please keep your seatbelt fastened at all times. Do not get up and walk around the plane. If you have to use the restroom, there is one in this part of the plane (point to the door of your room)." With the paper cup (oxygen mask) in your hand, say, "When we get up into, the air the cabin will be pressurized. If for some reason the cabin depressurizes, oxygen masks will drop from the ceiling above you." Hold up the cup/mask and let it drop, hanging by the string. Put it over your head as you continue: "Place the mask over your mouth and nose and breathe normally. If you are flying with children, put on your mask first, and then help the children." Put down the cup/mask and pick up the homemade safety information card. "Please review the information on your safety card."
- Announce that the plane is about to take off.
- Sit down and pretend to put on your seatbelt while the children pretend to put on their seatbelts, too.
- Imitate how the plane sounds when it taxis down the runway.
- Tell the children the plane has been cleared for take-off, then pretend to take off. Encourage the class to make loud engine noises, and act like you are being shoved back in your seat by the G-force of taking off.
- Wait a moment, then tell the children it is time for their on-board snack.
- Go around and serve the children the snack, telling them they can't get up because they are on an airplane and there isn't much room to walk around. Besides, the attendant has told them to remain in their seats unless they have to go to the restroom.

(continues)

Could I Get You a Pillow or Some Peanuts? (flight attendant) *(continued)*

- During the snack, discuss air travel and how to behave when flying.
- After the snack, pick up the trash like the flight attendant would.
- End this activity by telling the children you have reached your destination, and go through the landing routine with their participation in appropriate noises, etc.
- Tell them you like your job because you enjoy travel and seeing different places, and most of all, you like to serve and help people.

Practical Tips

- *Use this activity before summer vacation or a holiday when some children might be flying.*
- *Make this activity as short or as long as you want, depending upon the children's ages and interest.*
- *Extend the activity with an in-flight movie (a short cartoon).*
- *Do the activity prior to naptime, and pass out the children's blanket and pillow. (If you do this, you won't want the take-off to be quite as energetic!)*

Off We Go Into the Wild Blue Yonder (airplane pilot)

Objective
To learn about what a pilot does and become more comfortable with flying

Approximate Time
10–20 minutes

Ages
3–8

Materials
Pictures of planes
A suit jacket or uniform jacket, if available

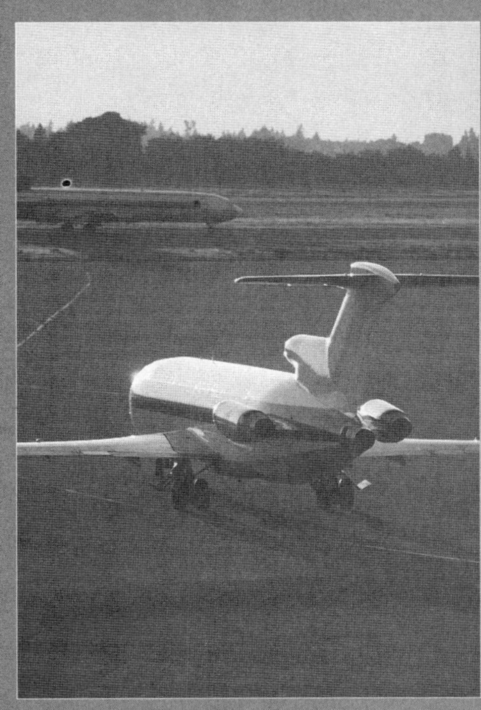

- Announce to the children that you are a guest airline pilot who has come to talk to them about airplanes and flying. Ask if any of them know someone who is an airplane pilot.
- Inform them that you are here today to teach them about a pilot's job.
- Tell them that one thing an airplane pilot has to do is to pack a really small suitcase, and have them begin to pack their imaginary suitcases—underwear for four days, a clean uniform, a shaving or make-up kit, pajamas, clothes to wear when not working, a book to read.
- Inform the children that you usually are gone for three or four days at a time before you come home for a few days, then leave for work again.
- Tell them you have learned how to manage the controls in the cockpit—the many different switches, buttons, and levers—and you have to know which ones to push and pull at which time.
- Ask the children to pretend to push and pull all kinds of buttons and levers, and ask them if they have ever been in the cockpit of a really big airplane.
- Tell them that pilots need to know how to take off and land the airplane, and demonstrate this. Let them have fun taking off and landing their big jets.

(continues)

Off We Go Into the Wild Blue Yonder (airplane pilot) *(continued)*

- Tell the children that being an airplane pilot is a wonderful job because you get to travel and you meet a lot of new people. Say that you enjoy your job because you like to help people go places while making them feel safe.

Practical Tips

- *As a companion to the flight attendant activity (Activity 75), take one role and enlist another teacher, with one of you as the flight attendant and the other as the pilot. The pilot could make announcements such as cruising altitude and weather in the destination city, and point out landmarks such as the Grand Canyon.*
- *Write to an airline explaining your activity and requesting "wing" pins for your class. The airline might offer pictures of the airplanes or other freebies as well.*

Objective
To learn about taxicabs and taxi drivers

Approximate Time
10–20 minutes

Ages
3–8

Materials
Chauffeur hat
Chairs set up in groups of four like an automobile
Play money

May I Give You a Lift? (cab driver)

- Tell the children that you are a taxi driver and you have been called to take them where they are going. Explain what a taxicab is to any of the children who do not know. Say something like, "A taxicab is a car or a van that someone drives to take people where they tell him to go."
- Ask them if they have ever ridden in a taxi, and invite those who have to tell the class about it.
- Ask the children where they would like to go. Have them get in your imaginary cab and take them for the ride—from one area of your building to another, or to the playground, or just around the room.
- When you get to the destination, tell them they have arrived and let them know what the "fare" is.
- Have one of them (or another teacher) pay you with the play money.

(continues)

May I Give You a Lift?
(cab driver) *(continued)*

Practical Tips

- *Tell the children about tipping, that they should give the driver a tip. For older children, explain that this is a percentage of the total and a minimum per person or suitcase.*
- *When using this activity, consider where your school is located. If the children you work with live in a city, they may be quite familiar with cabs and drivers. If they are from a small town or a more remote area, they may not have the same familiarity. Explain that children live in different places that aren't all the same as where we live. Some children live in large cities, where a lot of people take cabs, and other children live in small towns or the mountains or on farms, where people take cabs less often.*

78

The Wheels on the Bus . . . Are My Job (city bus driver)

Objective
To better understand the city bus driver's job and how to take buses

Approximate Time
10–20 minutes

Ages
3–8

Materials
Chauffeur hat (optional)
Chairs set up like a bus
Route schedule, real or handmade
Pay box of some kind and coin-type play money

- Inform the children that you are a city bus driver and have come to talk to them about public transportation, which is very important, especially in large cities.
- Explain the different types of public transportation—subways, streetcars, overhead rail systems, buses. Ask the children to tell you which types of public transportation they have taken.

- Talk about routes and schedules, and show examples, so they can better understand routes and public bus transportation.
- Tell them you are going to take them on your city bus to the downtown area to visit the city courthouse.
- Have them line up single file and tell them they need to get on the bus one at a time and put their token or coins in the pay box (explain that you always have to pay when you first get on the bus).
- After they have put their coins in the box, tell them to have a seat.

(continues)

The Wheels on the Bus . . . Are My Job (city bus driver) *(continued)*

- Explain that you have to make regularly scheduled stops on the route and they shouldn't get off until you get to the courthouse.
- Close the imaginary bus door, making the sound: CH>>>>>>>>>TCH.
- Pretend to drive around. When you go around a corner, lean to one side and get the children to lean with you.
- Make a stop every 20 seconds or so.
- When you apply the brake, lean forward, then back, like you would if you were really on a bus. Have the children lean with you.
- Each time you stop, announce the name of the bus stop: "We are at Fourth and Mulberry. Anyone getting off at Fourth and Mulberry?" Then make the sound of the doors opening: CH>>>>>>>>>TCH.
- Invite a volunteer to get on the bus, and say: "Hello. How are you today?" Watch as the "passenger" puts the fare into the box and turns around to find a seat.
- Close the door—CH>>>>>>>>>TCH—and drive to the next stop.
- Do this as many times as the children are interested before arriving at the chosen destination.
- Demonstrate how to pull the overhead cord to signal the driver when you want to get off. Make the "ding" sound.

(continu

The Wheels on the Bus . . . Are My Job (city bus driver) *(continued)*

Practical Tips

- *With older children, talk about transfer schedules and show some routes. Have them tell you how they would go about transferring.*
- *Also, with older children, use this activity to teach counting money, making change, and the like.*
- *Use this as an activity when you are getting ready to change areas: Line up the group in twos or threes and have them "ride" down the hall with you at the wheel.*
- *Use this activity before taking a fieldtrip to a museum or other place accessible by city bus (or use it in conjunction with a fieldtrip suggested in the Practical Tips for Activity 84, "How Fast Can You Type?").*

Come on Back . . . Okay . . . a Little More (garbage collector)

Objective
To learn what a sanitary engineer does and also about recycling

Approximate Time	Ages
10–20 minutes	3–8

Materials
Trash bags to line the containers
Leather gloves
Empty beverage cans, plastic bottles, and similar disposable containers

- Tell the children that you are a garbage collector and that your job is a lot more complicated than just picking up the trash. You also are involved in recycling.

- Explain that recycling means taking items that can be used again and again, first sorting them so they can go to different recycling plants. Bring up the different types of recyclables—glass, plastic, paper, etc. Explain that things that are recycled are not just washed out and refilled with new food and drink but actually are melted down and remade into new cans and bottles. The paper is cleaned up and made into brand new paper without any writing on it.
- Ask the children if their family is involved in recycling, and encourage them to get their family involved in doing this if they aren't already. Explain the recycling programs in your community.

(continu

Come on Back . . . Okay . . . a Little More (garbage collector) *(continued)*

- Throw something in the smallest wastebasket you have, and suggest that this may be like the one in their bathroom or bedroom at home.
- Ask the children what they would do with that wastebasket when it gets full. Lead them through the sequence: They put trash in their house in a wastebasket (usually), empty the wastebasket into a larger trash can in the house, and put those trash bags into an outdoor container or dumpster (show them the dumpster at your school).
- Ask the children to pretend that one of the larger cans is the outdoor trash container at their place, and ask them if they know what happens to it. Remind them that once a week the garbage collector picks it up (if that is the case).
- Dump the small wastebasket into one of the larger cans, then pull it over by the door to the room.
- Ask how many of them have seen the garbage truck pick up the trash. Playing the role of the trash collector, tell them that you go into a different neighborhood and pick up the trash every day, so you get around the neighborhood a lot.
- Ask them if they know where the trash goes after the truck picks it up. Explain that it goes to the city or county landfill (also known as "the dump"), a place where big earth-moving equipment is used to dig huge holes and bury the trash so it eventually will turn into dirt. This takes many years, and some plastics and other types of trash never turn into dirt—which is why we want to recycle.
- Tell the children you enjoy your job because you like working outdoors and get a sense of satisfaction from providing such an important service to people. Remind them that if you didn't do your job, all their trash would start piling up and it would get stinky and maybe make people sick.

(continues)

Come on Back . . . Okay . . . a Little More (garbage collector) *(continued)*

Practical Tips

- *Make arrangements to watch the trash collector empty your school's dumpster if this is done during the hours the children are there.*
- *Consider starting a recycling drive in your classroom for a few weeks or months to get the children conditioned to sorting trash according to the recycling guidelines in your community.*
- *When you are involved in this activity, have the children sing this song with you, to the tune of "The William Tell Overture":*

To the dump, to the dump, to the dump, dump, dump
To the dump, to the dump, to the dump, dump, dump
To the dump, to the dump, to the dump, dump, dump
To the dump, to the dump, dump, dump.

Big Wheels a' Rollin'—No, I mean BIG WHEELS (truck driver)

Objective
To find out what over-the-road truckers do

Approximate Time
10–20 minutes

Ages
3–8

Materials
Large toy trucks (preferably, a semi-truck and a tractor-trailer, if you can find them)
Cowboy boots

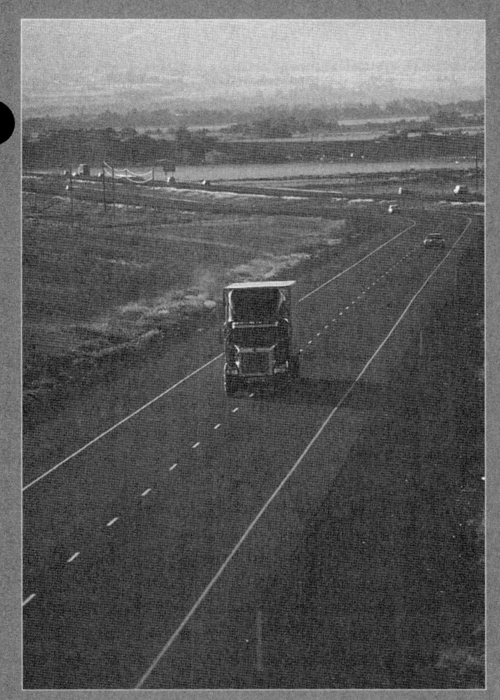

- Announce to the children that you are an over-the-road trucker. Ask them if they know anyone who drives a big truck, and encourage those who do to tell about the truck driver's work.
- Explain that you drive a large truck called a tractor—not the kind of tractor that plows fields but the front part of a truck that is also called a tractor (if you have the toy, show it to the children now). Tell the children that the tractor part pulls a trailer, so that's why it is called a tractor-trailer.
- Explain that all kinds of things are hauled across the nation in tractor-trailers, and this is how most things get to the store for us to buy.
- Look around the room and point out things that were delivered to the stores by truck—children's clothing, the carpet on the floor, the light fixtures, the sink, and so on. Tell them that almost everything in the grocery store got there because someone delivered it in a truck.
- Describe the different types of truck drivers:
  - Some are gone from home several days or weeks at a time and make long-distance trips, while others deliver things a few miles away and are home every night.

(continues)

Big Wheels a' Rollin'—No, I mean BIG WHEELS (truck driver) *(continued)*

- Some work for large companies, and others work for small companies, and still others drive their own truck and get delivery orders themselves.

- Tell the children that you enjoy your job as a truck driver because you like to travel and drive a huge truck. Also, you take pride in knowing that you help get things to the store for people to buy.
- Tell them you like to toot your horn for children when they give you the signal. Show the children the signal, and make the sound.

Practical Tips

- *If you don't know anyone who drives a truck, consider talking to one of the sales reps for a company that delivers goods to your school or center. Arrangements might be made for your class to look at one of their trucks close up.*

Fresh Bread (baker)

Objective
To learn about and practice one role of a baker

Approximate Time
10–20 minutes

Ages
3–6

Materials
Fresh bread and juice or milk for snack time
Mixing bowls (one per child)
Measuring cups and spoons enough to go around
Bread pans
Kitchen timer (optional)
Flour and water
An apron
A white chef's hat (if you can find it)

- Before snack time, put on the apron and the chef's hat, and tell the children you are here today to tell and show the class about your job as a baker.
- Inform them that bakers have been around for thousands of years. Ask those who have been to a bakery to name some of the foods they saw there—bread, doughnuts, cakes, pies, pastries, muffins, bagels, coffee cakes, cookies, etc. Tell them you make all kinds of baked foods.
- Announce that they are going to be your assistants today to help you make bread. Bring out the bowls and utensils, and the flour and container of water for yourself (and the children, if they are doing this).
- Demonstrate (and help them measure and mix the flour and water if applicable).
- When the mixture gets thick, take the large lump of dough out of your bowl and demonstrate how to knead it (have the children say the word "knead" with you). Real or imagined, this is a unique way for children to burn off some energy!
- Put the "bread" in the pan, and have the children do the same if they have really mixed the flour and water.

(continues)

ROLE-PLAY

Fresh Bread (baker) *(continued)*

- Tell the children the bread has to rise before you bake it. Set a kitchen timer for five minutes (or whatever length of time you want). Tell them it normally takes more than an hour for the dough to rise, but this dough is magic and will rise in a few minutes.
- Put the "risen" bread dough in the (imaginary) oven to bake and set the timer again. Tell the children it normally takes 30–45 minutes for bread to bake but because this bread is magic, it will be done much sooner.
- Bring out the real bread you have set aside for snacks, and give the children juice or milk to drink with it.
- Talk about the many different types of bread—rye, wheat, multi-grain, sourdough, and so on.
- Tell the children that people all over the world eat bread every day. This is a good chance to mention breads from different cultures—American Indian, Italian, Mexican, Jewish, German, etc.
- End this activity by telling the children how much you like the smell of newly baked bread and the compliments you get from those who eat it and the other things you make—"MMMmmm!"

Practical Tips

- *For older children, make a food activity out of their helping you actually make a loaf of bread.*

How Do You Like Your Steak? (chef)

Objective
To learn about what a chef or cook does

Approximate Time
10–20 minutes

Ages
3–8

Materials
Apron and chef's hat
Several cookbooks
Pots and pans
Mixing bowl
Whisk and large spoon

- Preferably, use this activity before a snack or meal.
- Put on the apron and hat and tell the children you are a famous chef and have come to give them a cooking demonstration.
- Ask the children if any of them know a chef or a cook. If so, ask them to tell about what that person does and what kind of food he or she prepares. (Ask if they have ever visited that person at work.)

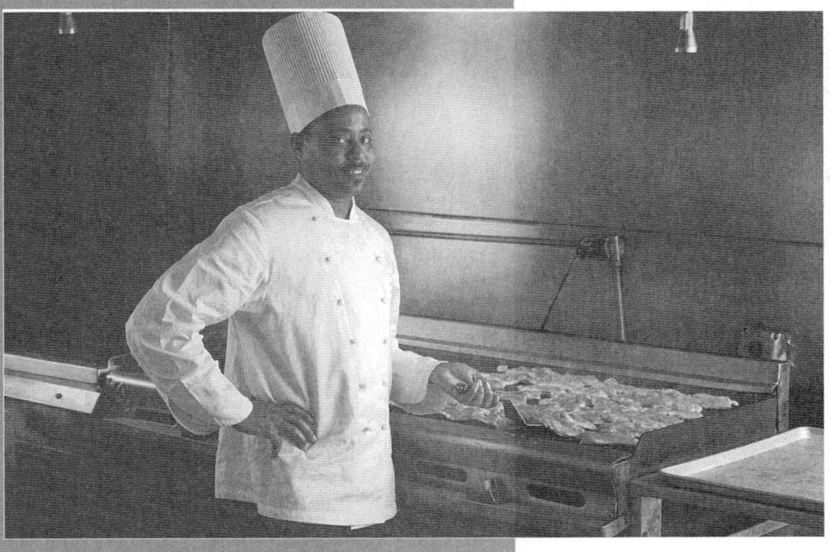

- Explain what you do, and say there are many different types of chefs or cooks—those who prepare food from only one culture, such as French or Italian, those who have a specialty such as desserts, those who work inside restaurants, and those who prepare food to take out.
- Tell the children that some chefs and cooks fix foods in exact amounts that have been ordered in advance (such as food for wedding receptions), while other cooks have a lot of different food ingredients on hand to cook to order because they don't know how many people will order anything.

(continues)

How Do You Like Your Steak? (chef) *(continued)*

- Begin your cooking demonstration: Take out the mixing bowl, and dump imaginary things into it. Stir or whip the imaginary ingredients.
- Tell the children what you are making and what each ingredient is as you add it. Use one of the cookbooks to read the ingredients and directions.
- Have volunteer-children help by dumping different ingredients into the mixing bowl as you call them out.
- Mix everything together and go through a cooking routine:
  - If you are using a frying pan, throw some imaginary food high in the air and catch it in the pan behind your back.
  - Bang the pans and spoons or the whisk and spoon against each other.
- When you finish, display your creation on an imaginary plate with a flourish. And don't forget the garnish!
- Pass around the fabulous creation and let the children each "sample" it.
- End the activity by telling the class that you like your job as a chef a lot because you get to be creative and make food that people like.

Practical Tips

- *When the children get their snack or lunch, have them pretend that they are eating what you fixed them in the demonstration.*
- *For older children, combine this activity with a real cooking activity in which the children actually cook something, using one of the many kid-friendly recipes available today.*

Coffee, Tea, or Milk? (food server)

Objective
To understand the job of a server

Approximate Time
10–20 minutes

Ages
3–8

Materials
Half-apron
Real restaurant menus
Pad and pencil to take an order
Tray
Paper plates and cups

- Use this activity before snack time and use the actual snacks as the "order." Pretend, for example, that the glass of milk for the snack is a large milkshake and the crackers are a hamburger and fries.
- Tell the children they are going to a restaurant to eat dinner. (Beforehand, you could let them choose which restaurant, as long as it's a sit-down-and-be-waited-on type of restaurant.)
- Have the children line up outside the classroom door. As they enter the room, act as the hostess and say something like, "Table for [12] . . . yes, follow me this way." Lead them around some obstacles (tables of people already eating) in the room.
- When they arrive at their table—which could be a table-type formation on the floor or actual tables—wait for them to be seated, then give each of them a menu and tell them their server will be right there to take their drink order.
- Walk to the other side of the room and put on the half-apron.
- When you come back to them, use a different voice to introduce yourself: "I'll be your server today. May I get you a beverage?"

(continues)

ROLE-PLAY

Coffee, Tea, or Milk?
(food server) *(continued)*

- If you have a large class with more than one teacher or aides, divide the class into groups and each of you "work" your own imaginary restaurant table. Or have a few children act as servers-in-training, who will assist with this "large party."
- Have each member of the group tell you what he or she wants to order from the menu. (The children don't actually have to be able to read the menu, just look at it and pretend.)
- Walk to the other side of the room, turn around, and come back with your tray of drinks (paper cups). Pass out the drinks while you name them—and see if you can get the right drink to the right person!
- Now take their food orders (let them each order something, but don't let them drag it out too long as they tend to do), and after each one gives you an order, say something like, "That's an excellent choice, sir. Would you like mashed potatoes with that?" (or whatever seems appropriate).
- After writing the orders on the pad, go to your imaginary kitchen and give the orders to the cook, saying things like, "Hold the mayo on the BLT" and "Make those mashed dusty and hold the P and O from the 72."
- After you finish giving the order, stack the paper plates up and down your arms, on one knee, even on top of your head.
- Bring the imaginary food to the table and pass out the orders. Use this as a memory exercise to ask the children to help you remember who ordered what.
- Then pass out the real snacks.

(continue

Coffee, Tea, or Milk? (food server) *(continued)*

- End the activity by telling the children you like being a server a lot because you enjoy meeting people and you like to play a mental game of trying to anticipate what people will order.
- Mention that part of your pay comes from tips—money people leave on the table after you serve them.

Practical Tips

- *For older children and those who comprehend the concept of percentage, explain that the customary tip is a percentage of the total cost of the meal or a minimum per person at the table.*

How Fast Can You Type? (administrative assistant/ secretary)

Objective
To learn about the tasks of an administrative assistant or secretary

Approximate Time	**Ages**
5–10 minutes	3–8

Materials
A pretend computer
Legal pad and pen or pencil
A play telephone

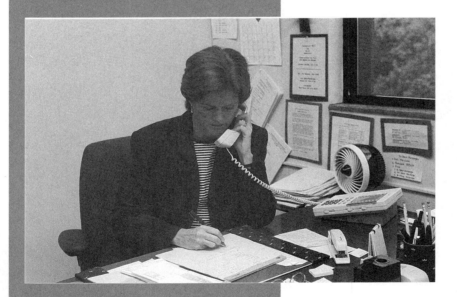

- Tell the children you are visiting today so they can learn what you do for a living. Have them try to guess what it is.
- Give them hints: "I work in an office. Sometimes I answer the phone, but I have more duties than a receptionist. I use a computer, and I write letters. Sometimes I make appointments for my boss. I research information for projects for my boss, and sometimes I make reports. I also must keep things in the office neat and organized and filed away so we can find it later. I go to meetings and take notes for other people."
- Encourage the children to ask questions to figure out what you do.

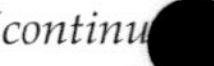
(continu

How Fast Can You Type? (administrative assistant/secretary) *(continued)*

- Once they figure out what your job is, ask if any of them has a parent or relative who is an administrative assistant or secretary. If so, invite them to tell what they know about this job.
- End this activity by telling the children you enjoy working in an office, using the computer, and keeping things organized. You feel good about helping your boss be more effective and not missing meetings or commitments, and you like helping people to be successful.

Practical Tips

- *Use this activity in preparation for a fieldtrip to an office that has a secretary or an administrative assistant who would be willing to show the children around and explain his or her job (maybe one of the children's parents or friends could help to arrange this).*
- *Combine the fieldtrip with the one suggested in the Practical Tips for "The Wheels on the Bus . . . Are My Job" (Activity 78).*

Vote for Me—I'm a Nice Guy (politician)

Objective
To learn about politics and politicians

Approximate Time
5–10 minutes

Ages
4–10

Materials
Political campaign posters and materials
An American flag
. . . and a firm handshake

- Tell the children you are a politician and you are here today to earn their votes.
- Have them all sit down, and begin your speech:
  - Tell them you are concerned about the same things they are.
  - Make campaign promises (longer lunches, shorter naps, all the toys they need, and so on).
- At this point, the children probably will be befuddled and still not know what a politician is, so stop and ask if they can tell you. (You might get some wild answers.)
- Explain that the United States is a democracy, which means that people vote in elections and make laws that tell us to do certain things. Politicians from the President to the county dog catcher all need the most votes to get elected to do their jobs.
- Explain what "election" and "candidate" mean. Tell the children that different people decide they can do a better job than someone else and try to get people to vote for them.
- Use the example of the class needing a sheriff: Both Katie and Billy decide we should vote for them, so they each try to convince us who would be best. Katie might say she was the sheriff in her old class so she knows more about it, while Billy

(continue

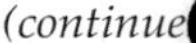

Vote for Me—I'm a Nice Guy (politician) *(continued)*

might tell us it is time for change and he has new ideas. Then we would have an election and those who want to vote will do so. At the end of the election, we count the votes. The winner is the one with the most votes.

- End this activity by telling the children that a lot of people want to be politicians because they like to help people and hope to make their community (name their city or town) or state, or country a better place.

Practical Tips

- *Get some leftover campaign literature from your local political parties—making sure not to "play favorites."*
- *Get in touch with the League of Women Voters to obtain information about elections and registering to vote.*

ROLE-PLAY

Your Honor, My Client Is Innocent! (Attorney/Judge)

OBJECTIVE
To begin to learn about the legal system and courts

APPROXIMATE TIME
10–20 minutes

AGES
4–10

MATERIALS
Choir robe or graduation gown that could pass for a judge's robe
Gavel
Briefcase
File folders with papers inside

- Put on your robe and ask the children if they have ever seen any of the court shows on TV or if any of them has been in a courtroom. Listen to their responses.
- Tell them you are here today to talk about what happens in a courtroom because you are an attorney—someone who will help when we have a problem involving a law or need advice about something that involves laws.
- Inform them that many things require an attorney—buying a new house, making a business decision, getting a divorce, and so on.
- Say that, as an attorney, you have to have a lot of education and follow many rules. For example:
  - What you wear: All attorneys, male and female, must wear a business suit.
  - How you talk and approach your case: Who talks when, how attorneys refer to each other and the judge, and so on.

(continue

ROLE-PLAY

Your Honor, My Client Is Innocent! (Attorney/Judge) *(continued)*

- Conclude by saying how much you like your work as an attorney because you are an expert and you like to do research (find information in books) and help people in tight spots.

Practical Tips

- *Even though divorce may be a touchy subject, consider it as a realistic topic to be prepared to discuss with children. When talking about a sensitive subject like this, avoid giving your own opinions or generalizing. Just listen, and let the children talk. Your role is to support the children, not complicate their thinking and emotions.*

This Was a Good Person (funeral home director)

Objective
To introduce the concept of death from the perspective of a funeral director

Approximate Time
5–10 minutes

Ages
6–10

Materials
An obituary from the newspaper
A printed remembrance from a funeral

- Tell the children you are a visiting funeral director and you are there to answer their questions and help them understand what happens at a funeral.
- Ask the children if any of them has been to a funeral. Encourage anyone who has to talk about it with the class. Because funerals can be traumatic for children, this activity might be especially helpful to a child who has gone to a funeral or has had to face the death of a family member.

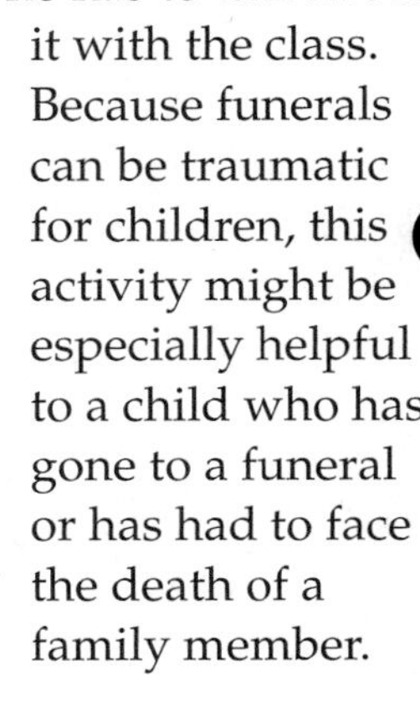

- Explain that at some funerals people come and look at the body of the person who just died. At other funerals the casket that holds the body is closed.

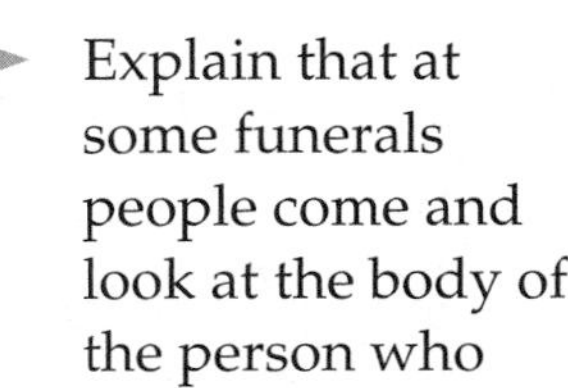

- Tell them that when someone dies, someone calls you and asks you to pick up the person's body and prepare the body for the funeral.

(continu

This Was a Good Person (funeral home director) *(continued)*

- Say that another thing you do is to meet with the family and talk about what the family members want the funeral to be like—for different people to talk about the person who died, to have singing or other music, to have someone read a story about the person's life—that sort of thing.
- Tell them that as the funeral director, you also help the family pick out a casket (explain what it is and maybe show a picture), which goes in a *limousine* to a cemetery.
- Explain that the people gather at the cemetery near the place where the casket will be put into the ground, and they say more good things about the person before they leave the cemetery.
- Conclude this activity by telling the children your job as a funeral director is important because you help people during the sad time after someone has died.

Practical Tips

- *Because this is a sensitive subject, approach the topic of death with caution and tact. With the approval of your school or center and the parents, you may be able to teach even young children about the concept of death in a way that will help allay their fears.*
- *Be aware of family circumstances of the children in your group and be available to listen to children who are experiencing a traumatic situation such as a death in the family.*

Where Do You Want Those Trees? (Landscape Designer)

Objective
To learn what a landscape architect or designer does

Approximate Time
5–15 minutes

Ages
3–8

Materials
Blueprints (Activity 67, "My House Needs To Be Fixed," may be helpful here)
Shovel
Rake
Gloves
Notebook and pencil

- Tell the children you are a landscape designer and are here to help them plan their yard and garden.
- Ask for a volunteer to be your assistant. Have the volunteer come up and hold the shovel or rake.
- Ask the rest of the children to sit down so they can all hear and watch you and your assistant.
- Tell the children that you and your new helper are going to walk around the "yard" (the classroom) and suggest where to put trees, bushes, and other plants.
- Have your assistant and the class make suggestions about what to plant, while you take notes and nod like you are considering their suggestions.
- Get out your blueprints and talk about pretend things in the yard (for example, "Look—here's the school, and here's the street. This circle represents the tree that's already out there. It sounds like you're suggesting that we plant a bush here and put in a small fruit tree here. I would recommend using ivy as a ground cover here and small rocks over here for contrast," and so on.

(continue

ROLE-PLAY

Where Do You Want Those Trees? (Landscape Designer) *(continued)*

- Inform the children that you and your assistant will send some workers over with trucks and equipment to move some dirt and plant those trees.
- End this activity by telling the children your job as a landscape designer is rewarding because you like to see things grow, you enjoy being outdoors, and you get a lot of satisfaction from seeing your drawing come to life in someone's yard.

Practical Tips

- *Instead of doing this activity inside, do it outside and actually walk around and look at real plants and places where you could plant a bush or a tree.*
- *If it's okay with your school principal or center director, sponsor a plant or tree in the schoolyard.*
- *Call or write to the National Arbor Day Foundation for information on the usefulness and care of various trees and plants.*

89

Red Curtains Will Look Just Right (interior designer)

Objective
To understand the role of an interior designer

Approximate Time
5–15 minutes

Ages
3–8

Materials
A set of blueprints (see "My House Needs To Be Fixed," Activity 67)
Paint chip cards
Wallpaper sample books
Fabric swatches

- Tell the children that you are an interior designer and you have been called to suggest ways to redecorate the classroom.
- Ask the class if anyone has had an interior designer come to their house to help them decide how to decorate their home. Have anyone who responds tell about the experience.
- Explain to the group that an interior designer helps people decorate the inside of their home. This means painting or hanging wallpaper and choosing furniture and other things to create a certain feeling or mood. Sometimes the interior designer even suggests remodeling something, like moving a wall.
- Bring out the blueprints and inform the children that you will consult these as you plan the changes.
- Show them the paint chips and have them suggest colors they like.
- Show them wallpaper books, and have them try to agree on one or more patterns for different rooms.
- Show them the fabric swatches and have them pick out material for the new sofa (you might want to circulate all the paint chip, wallpaper, and fabric samples simultaneously so all the children will have something to focus on without waiting).

(continue

Red Curtains Will Look Just Right (interior designer) *(continued)*

- Inform them that you will have a crew of people coming to help with the actual redecorating.
- End this activity by telling the children you like your job a lot because you enjoy planning the changes and seeing how much better the rooms look after the redecorating. Tell them you chose interior design as a career because you like to work with fabric, paint, and colors and are good at coming up with themes and matching furniture.

Practical Tips

- *If you have already done any of the previous activities involving blueprints, ask the children if they can remember another job that uses blueprints.*

How Many Hats Does a Farmer Wear?

OBJECTIVE
To learn about farms—where cereal, meat, wool, eggs, milk, wool, fruit and vegetables, and many other products come from

APPROXIMATE TIME
5–15 minutes

AGES
3–6

MATERIALS
Optometrist's hat with the light on a band around it
Hard hat
Mechanic's cap
Chef's hat
Ranger's hat

- Introduce yourself as a farmer and tell the children you are here to talk to them about what you do for a living.
- Ask the children if they know anyone who is a farmer or a rancher, and ask them what they think a farmer does for a living. Tell them you have come to describe what you do every day—except that all of your days are different. As you go through the following, put on whichever hat applies. Some days you put on your:
    - Veterinarian's hat (the one with the light band) because you have to tend to sick animals or help to deliver new baby animals.
    - Hard hat because you have to figure out how to build a new barn or a fence or dig ditches so the water will drain away instead of flooding.
    - Mechanic's hat because some days you have to operate big trucks and tractors or repair them when they break down.

(continued)

ROLE-PLAY

How Many Hats Does a Farmer Wear? *(continued)*

- Nutritionist's hat (chef's hat) because you have to make sure that your animals are eating the right kind of food to keep the animals healthy.
- Forest ranger's hat because you need to know about plants you grow and trees near your farm and be able to put out fires and keep your soil from being washed or blown away (introduce the term "erosion" if the children are old enough to comprehend the concept).

Imaginary hats, among others, might be:

- A scientist's hat because you have to understand what kinds of chemicals and other things are in your soil so your plants will grow and your animals will be safe.
- A weather forecaster's hat because you have to understand what sun and rain and other weather (such as wind and hail) will do to your plants, and you have to be able to tell when a storm is coming so you can protect your animals and your farm buildings.

► Finish this activity by reminding the children that farmers do a lot more than just milk cows and grow corn. They also run a business, keep their animals safe and healthy, know how to grow safe plants for food, understand the environment and the weather, and take care of their equipment and buildings.

(continues)

ROLE-PLAY

How Many Hats Does a Farmer Wear? *(continued)*

Practical Tips

- *If you live in a rural community, arrange a fieldtrip to a local farm so the children can see firsthand some of the things a farmer does (tell the farmer about the hats in this activity so he or she can elaborate or be more specific about this particular farm).*
- *If your school or center is in a more suburban or urban area, show any of a number of good children's videos that show farm life. Doing this would change it from a transition, but that's fine. (although it wouldn't be a transition activity anymore, which is ok!).*

Note: The information in this activity was adapted from the *Field Guide to Utah Agriculture in the Classroom* with permission from the Cooperative Extension Office, Utah State University.

Adapted from FFA® Food for America with permission from the National FFA Organization, 2005.

I Wouldn't Put a Wall There (architect)

Objective
To better understand what an architect does

Approximate Time
10–20 minutes

Ages
3–6

Materials
Architectural drawings
Chalkboard, posterboard, or butcher paper

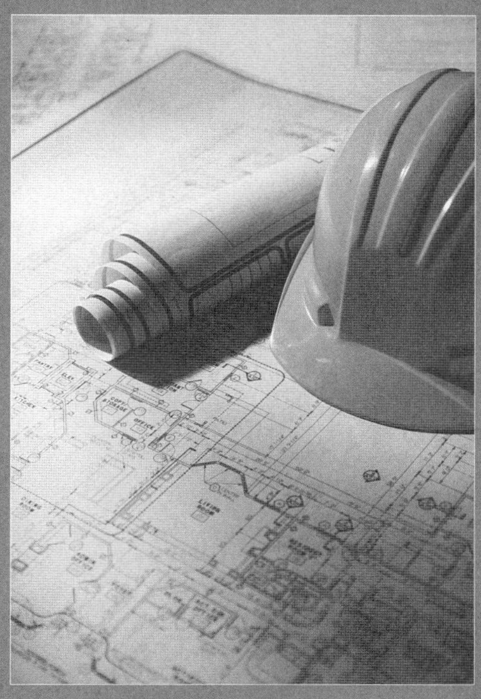

- Inform the children that you are an architect who has been invited to visit the class. Ask the children if they know what an architect does. After they have responded, tell them that an architect is actually a type of artist.
- Ask them if they know what makes someone an artist. Say that an artist is someone who creates pictures, music, poems, or sculptures from an original idea.
- Tell them that the art you create is in the form of buildings, and help them understand that architects design buildings for function, beauty, and safety.
- Tell them that you work on big drawing boards and use rulers and other tools to create drawings that the builders will understand and know how to make our buildings safe. Explain that architects also use computer programs to produce drawings. If you have actual architectural drawings, show them to the children.
- Draw a basic sketch of a house exterior on the chalkboard or on posterboard, and ask the children to help you decide where to put the walls, doors, and windows.

(continues)

I Wouldn't Put a Wall There (architect) *(continued)*

Practical Tips

- *If you have actual blueprints, have the children look them over. Talk about the different types of blueprints needed for different projects.*
- *Turn this activity into a group motor skills activity by having the children use blocks to try to build something according to a design they did.*

ROLE-PLAY

Imagination

The activities in this category:

Are suggested for teacher and students and for parents and children.

- Lead the children into an imaginary world where anything is possible.
- Are limited only by the ability to "get out of the box"—imagine, pretend, be goofy.
- Rarely need props—and actually discourage props for this category because it emphasizes imagination.

93

We're Going to the Store

Objective
To be involved in pretending

Approximate Time
10–20 minutes

Ages
3–6

Materials
NONE
(Optional: chair)

- Begin this activity by telling the children, "We're going to the grocery store to buy some things for lunch."
- Have the children get in a row or a circle.

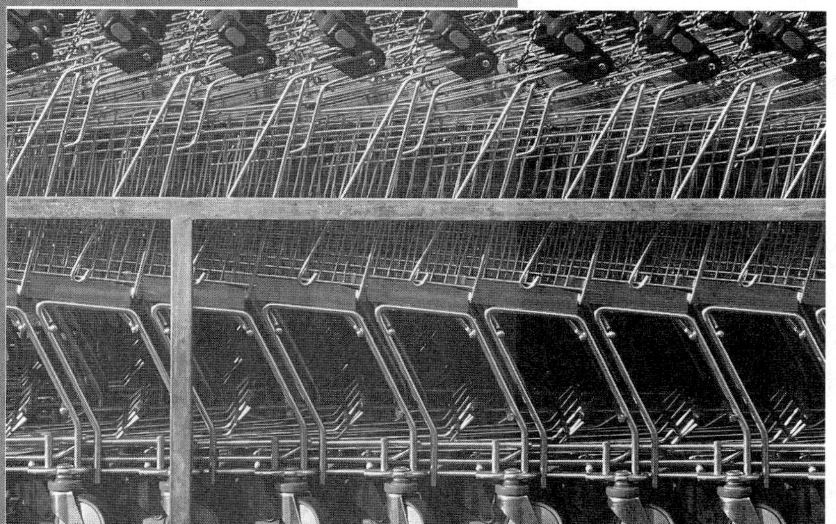

- Tell the children that "we're going to get in the car and drive to the store." Walk (in place) to the car, get in, and shut the door (this is where you could use a chair, but it isn't necessary).
- Make sure they are all fastened in their seatbelts before you turn the key and push your foot on the gas pedal.
- Have the children make the noise of the engine starting.
- Put the car in gear and drive to the store, mentioning things you see on the way (school playground, mall, etc.).
- Pull into the grocery store parking lot, park the car, shut off the engine, and unfasten your seatbelt.
- Open the door, step out of the car, and everybody walk (in place) to the store.
- Step up and wait for the automatic doors to open. Make the sound of the doors opening and

(continues)

We're Going to the Store *(continued)*

move your hands as if they are the doors opening, then closing.

- Get a cart and push it through the store.
- Ask the children what we should buy, and when they name an item, go to that aisle and pick it out.
- After getting the groceries, go to the check-out counter, where the clerk rings up your items.
- Pay for your groceries, carry them to the car, and load the trunk.
- Get in the car (don't forget your seatbelt) and repeat the driving routine to get you back home.
- End this activity by arriving back at school, or continue by bringing the groceries in the house and putting them away.

Practical Tips

- *Throughout this activity, keep the children involved by asking them what should happen next, and have them perform the actions along with you.*
- *Combine this activity with a memory activity by listing all the items you bought and asking the children to repeat them.*
- *Go through the routine of cooking, setting the table, eating, doing the dishes, and so on.*
- *Capitalize on children's vivid imagination to keep them entertained. An activity like this opens the door to other possibilities such as going out to eat (the list could go on and on).*
- *Ask your local grocery store manager about giving the children a tour, and do this activity prior to going on the fieldtrip to help prepare them.*

Objective
To practice pretending and also learn to differentiate animals

Approximate Time
5–10 minutes

Ages
3–6

Materials
NONE

If You Were an Animal, What Would You Be?

- Do this activity in the car or walking down the hall.
- After you have the children's attention, ask them: "If you were an animal, what would you be?"
- Give them time to think, then have them answer one by one (typical answers are monkey, doggie, elephant).
- Ask them for specifics about the animal they've chosen: "What sound does it make? How does it move?" etc.
- Have the child make noises like that animal.
- Invite them to choose another animal, and ask them about the sound this one makes, how it moves, and so on.
- Be sure to act along with them. They like you to be involved.

Practical Tips

- *If you try this activity while taking a class down the hall, let the children crawl on all fours like puppies, or be elephants with their arm raising up and down like a trunk.*

We're Going to Work

Objective
To practice pretending and better understand what parents do when they go to work

Approximate Time
10–20 minutes

Ages
3–7

Materials
NONE
(Optional: dress-up clothes)

- Tell the children, "We're going to be like our mom or dad today." Let the children decide which parent they want to emulate.
- Tell them they are getting dressed to go to work, so they should pick out something from the dress-up area that is like what their mom or dad wears to work.
- Have them get in their imaginary cars and drive to work (they might want to pretend to stop by the center or school and drop themselves off!).
- Tell the children they are coming into the parking lot where mom or dad works and they are going to park their car and walk into the building.
- Ask them what they do at their job, then have them go to an area of the room and pretend to do that kind of work (some might need some direction or suggestions, but most will be able to get started).
- Have the children "work" awhile, take a lunch break, then return to work.
- When the day is done, show them how mom or dad goes to the parking lot, gets in the car, puts on the seatbelt, starts the car, and drives to pick them up on the way home.
- With older children, have a circle-time discussion on what kinds of work their parents do.

(continue

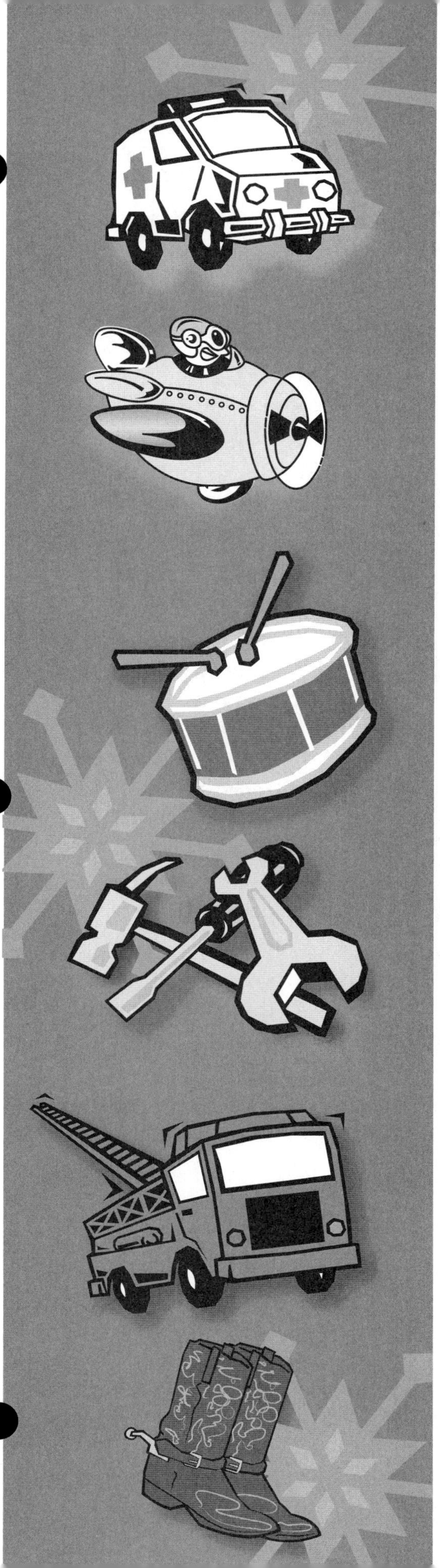

Practical Tips

- *Consider arranging a fieldtrip to where one or more of the parents work. You might be able to visit two or three in the same trip if they are close to one another or in the same company, and if the children are of an age to do this comfortably.*

Let's Ride the Subway

Objective
To learn about what a subway train is and how it works

Approximate Time
5–15 minutes

Ages
3–10

Materials
NONE

- Tell the children that your car broke down and you have to find a way to get to work.
- Brainstorm with the children different ways to get there (they might suggest taking a taxi or a bus, calling a friend, walking, etc.).

- If they do not suggest the subway (typically, if they don't live in a city with a subway, they won't think of this), discuss the various ideas and decide on the subway.
- Explain the subway to the children as a train that is underground.
- Have the children stand up and walk (in place) to the subway station.
- Walk down imaginary stairs into an underground tunnel, and describe how big the tunnel is and how many people are down there.
- Have the children look around and talk about what might be in the tunnel.
- Select a volunteer to be the ticket seller, and have the others check their pockets for money to buy their tickets (because you must have a ticket to ride the subway).

(continu

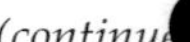

Let's Ride the Subway *(continued)*

- When everyone has a ticket, walk over to the subway loading zone.
- Stand back while the subway train pulls in and wait for it to come to a complete stop. Make the sound of the subway stopping—"pshhhhhhh."
- After the doors open, wait for the people to get off, then hurry to get on.
- Try to find a place to sit. There aren't enough seats for everyone, so you'll have to hold on to one of the poles.
- Get ready for the subway train to move on. Make the noise of the train starting to move.
- As you ride along, look out the windows and comment on how fast everything is going by ("Wow—we're going super fast on the subway!").
- When the subway train stops, have the children exit through the turnstile (you could act like the turnstile by standing with a hand extended that each child must push to pass through).

Practical Tips

- *If you live in a town or city without a subway, get some pictures (from the library or elsewhere) of a subway prior to doing the activity so the children will be better able to imagine what it is and help spark their interest in this activity.*

Let's Take a Taxi to the Airport

Objective
To plan a far-away trip and imagine calling a taxi to go to the airport

Approximate Time
3–8 minutes

Ages
3–8

Materials
NONE

- Tell the children you are going on a trip very far away.
- Ask them how they are going to get there and encourage them to brainstorm and shout out ideas until they say "an airplane!"

- Say, "Yes, an airplane will take you far away, but how do you get to the airport?" Suggest that they call a taxi. Explain that when people don't want to drive themselves, or if they don't have a car, they sometimes call a taxi to take them where they want to go, and they pay for the ride.
- Have the children pick up their imaginary phone and dial the taxi: 555-TAXI.
- Talk into your imaginary phone, then have the children repeat what you say: "Hello. My name is ____ and I want to go to the airport. I need someone to pick me up."
- Listen to the person on the other end of the phone, and answer, "You can be here in five minutes? Okay! Thanks." Then hang up.
- Then say, "You need to get ready for your trip. What should you take on your trip?
- Listen to the children's responses, and have them pretend to pack their suitcase.

(continu

Let's Take a Taxi to the Airport *(continued)*

- Have the children set their imaginary suitcases by the door.
- Have the children listen and look for the taxi.
- When it arrives, pick up the suitcase, get in the taxi, and tell the driver where you want to go: "To the airport."
- Wait for the taxi driver to drive for a short time, then tell the driver, "I'll get out here."
- Ask the driver how much you owe. Have the children dig in their pockets to pay the driver the $20 fare plus tip—extra money because the driver was so nice and helpful.
- Thank the driver, grab your suitcases, and run into the airport: "Come on—we don't want to miss our flight!"

Practical Tips

- *Do this activity in conjunction with "Could I Get You a Pillow or Some Peanuts?" (Activity 75)*
- *Do a learning series on transportation applicable to different age groups, which would take the activity out of the realm of a transition but would be of high interest.*
- *Use this activity to open up a discussion about "stranger danger." Remind the children not to get in the car with a stranger, even if he or she is driving a taxi, unless a parent (or someone like a parent) is with you.*
- *Use this activity to broaden children's understanding of the taxi as a mode of transportation, which will help to dispel any fears they might have about the unknown.*

Tell Me How To Get to Grandma's House

Objective
To use imagination and memory skills

Approximate Time
5–20 minutes

Ages
3–7

Materials
NONE

- Tell the children you're getting ready to go on a big trip, and it's going to be fun—but you need them to help you know how to get there.
- Have the children sit in a circle or against the wall.

- Ask the children how many of them have a grandma.
- Tell them you want to visit your own grandma but you can't remember how to get there. Maybe they can help you remember.
- Look around the room and ask a child (who likes to talk) how he or she gets to Grandma's house. Encourage the child to recount as many details as possible. This is a great time to get children to use their imagination to describe how to get there.
- Encourage younger children to get started by telling how you get to your own Grandma's house.
- Allow each child enough time to tell the group how to get to Grandma's house.

(continue

Tell Me How To Get to Grandma's House *(continued)*

Practical Tips

- *Use this activity to encourage children to talk and to be the center of attention. It makes them feel special, especially when they can talk about a family member or a trip they've taken.*
- *Set a good example for all the children by listening politely as each child speaks.*
- *Have the children come to the front of the class, as this makes them feel special and teaches the others that they should be listening because this is the only child who should be talking.*

Where's My Chicken?

Objective
To imagine where the chicken is hidden and have fun!

Approximate Time
7–15 minutes

Ages
3–7

Materials
A rubber or plastic chicken or a picture of a chicken

- Before the activity begins, hide the chicken somewhere in the room in a not-so-obvious but also not-so-hidden spot.
- Assemble the children and tell them someone has hidden the chicken and you need their help to find it.
  - Tell them you will count to three, and then they should get up and run to try to find it.
  - Count to three, then gradually give them general hints if they struggle to find the hidden chicken.
  - When someone finds the chicken, have all the children run back and sit in their original places.
  - If time permits, repeat the activity as often as it maintains the children's interest.

(continu
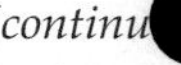

Where's My Chicken? *(continued)*

Practical Tips

- *Instead of hiding the chicken in advance, have the children cover their eyes while you hide the chicken. Walk around the room rustling things to confuse the children.*
- *Have the children count to three with you.*
- *Use something other than a rubber chicken to do this activity—something flexible and roughly the size of your open hand.*
- *Hide a different object each time you do this activity.*

100

Just a Minute . . . I'm in the Shower

Objective
To use imagination while learning about personal hygiene and human body parts

Approximate Time
5–7 minutes

Ages
3–7

Materials
NONE

- Do this activity particularly with younger children after having come in from outside.
- Tell them that their parents are coming soon, so they need to get cleaned up.
- Have all the children stand in a circle.

- Ask them to pick up their bar of soap (imaginary, of course), hold it up, and get ready to scrub off the dirt.
- Have them wash their hands (demonstrate by pretending to scrub your hands with your imaginary soap, and the children will mirror you).
- Have them scrub their feet after you demonstrate how to do that. Again, the children will mirror you.
- Continue by having them scrub their arms, legs, face, ears, belly, neck, armpits, knees, shoulders, back. . . .
- When they're finished with the imaginary soap, have them set it down on the floor.
- Have them get their imaginary shampoo, squirt some into their hands, rub their hands together to make shampoo bubbles, and then scrub their hair (show them by rubbing your imaginary shampoo on your head).

(contin

Just a Minute . . . I'm in the Shower *(continued)*

- Ask the children if they should rinse the soap off. They'll probably say "yes," so have them turn on an imaginary shower and dance around under the water (demonstrate this for them as well).
- Turn off the water, and ask the children what they should do next. Because they're wet, tell them they need to dry off.
- Have them use their imaginary towels to begin drying off. Tell them to make sure they get completely dry, and remind them to dry certain body parts such as their feet, knees, shoulders, and ears.
- After you name each body part, give them time to figure out where it is and towel it off.
- When they're completely dried off, have them throw you their imaginary towels and announce that they're ready to go home.
- When they're really ready to be picked up and go home, have them really wash their hands.

Practical Tips

- *Keep in mind that children will mimic you, so you'll want to be enthusiastic and exaggerate your motions. Overacting ensures that the children will mirror your enthusiasm and excitement about the activity. They children will be only as imaginative and excited as you encourage them to be by the tone you set.*

Your Turn

Use what you've learned to this point to add your own activities to the list. Keep in mind the categories of:

- Large and small motor skills
- Singing with or without actions
- Quiet down/crowd control
- Recognition/memory
- Repetition
- Character sketch/role-play
- Imagination

Have fun!

Your Turn

Category: ______________________________

Title: ______________________________

Objective: ______________________________

Approximate Time: ______________________________

Ages: ______________________________

Required Materials: ______________________________

Practical Tips